RICHARD BRAUTIGAN

"In general, people who write or talk about Brautigan tend to be either snidely patronizing or vacuously adoring. Most of his reviewers damn him with the faint praise of words like 'sweet' and 'gentle'; many of the students I've discussed Brautigan with say he's groovy and let it go at that. I think both of these responses are unfair to Brautigan's work. I'll try to take a good steady look at Brautigan's books, without either condescension or adulation, and to show what he's trying to say and how he's trying to say it."—from *Richard Brautigan,* by Terence Malley.

Richard Brautigan is the second volume in an exciting series of critical appreciations called *WRITERS FOR THE SEVENTIES.*

WRITERS FOR THE SEVENTIES

Kurt Vonnegut, Jr. by Peter J. Reed

Richard Brautigan by Terence Malley

Hermann Hesse by Edwin F. Casebeer

J.R.R. Tolkien by Robley Evans

General Editor: Terence Malley,
Long Island University

RICHARD BRAUTIGAN

by

Terence Malley

Long Island University (Brooklyn Center)

WARNER
PAPERBACK LIBRARY
NEW YORK

WARNER PAPERBACK LIBRARY EDITION
First Printing: October, 1972

ACKNOWLEDGMENTS

From *In Watermelon Sugar* by Richard Brautigan. Copyright © 1968 by Richard Brautigan. A Seymour Lawrence Book/Delacorte Press. Reprinted by permission of the publisher.

From *Rommel Drives on Deep into Egypt* by Richard Brautigan. Copyright © 1970 by Richard Brautigan. A Seymour Lawrence Book/Delacorte Press. Reprinted by permission of the publisher.

From *Trout Fishing in America* by Richard Brautigan. Copyright © 1967 by Richard Brautigan. A Seymour Lawrence Book/Delacorte Press. Reprinted by permission of the publisher.

From *The Pill Versus the Springhill Mine Disaster* by Richard Brautigan. Copyright © 1968 by Richard Brautigan. A Seymour Lawrence Book/Delacorte Press. Reprinted by permission of the publisher.

From *The Abortion* by Richard Brautigan. Copyright © 1970, 1971 by Richard Brautigan. Reprinted by permission of Simon and Schuster.

From *Revenge of the Lawn* by Richard Brautigan. Copyright © 1963, 1964, 1965, 1966, 1967, 1969, 1970, 1971 by Richard Brautigan. Reprinted by permission of Simon and Schuster.

From *A Confederate General from Big Sur* by Richard Brautigan. Grove Press, Inc. Copyright © 1964 by Richard Brautigan. Reprinted by permission of the author and his agent, The Sterling Lord Agency, Inc.

Warner Paperback Library is a division of Warner Books, Inc., 315 Park Avenue South, New York, N.Y. 10010.

For Bruce Silverman, Howie Menikoff, Joe Ornstein, and Milton Batalion—former students, who stumbled me on to Brautigan in the first place.

WRITERS FOR THE SEVENTIES
Richard Brautigan

Foreword.
Richard Brautigan:
A Writer for the Seventies

Richard Brautigan is one volume in a series of critical appreciations under the collective title, "Writers for the Seventies." Other books in this series are *Kurt Vonnegut, Jr.,* by Peter J. Reed; *Hermann Hesse,* by Edwin F. Casebeer; and *J.R.R. Tolkien,* by Robley Evans. The intention of these studies is to provide clear and balanced discussions of the main themes and techniques of the four authors in question. In each case, the critic has avoided excessively technical, academic terminology. In general, the four critics have addressed their subjects directly or even personally, without the sort of detachment that makes so many critical studies seem remote. Hopefully, the volumes in the Writers for the Seventies series will serve as good introductions to the four authors under discussion, for readers only slightly familiar with their books, while offering fresh insights for those who have already read the major works of Brautigan, Vonnegut, Hesse, and Tolkien.

A second—less direct—intention of the Writers for the Seventies series is to help, in a small way, to bridge that large and apparently increasing gap between the high school and college age readers of today and their parents and/or teachers. Each of the critics involved in this project is a youngish professor at an American college. All four are in their thirties: old enough to have had their graduate training in what seems already, only ten or twelve years later, a time of relatively settled, traditional standards; young enough to feel the impact of today's counter culture and to be aware of their students' insistence on "relevance" in literature. In each volume, the emphasis is on critical *appreciation;* in each case, the critic tries to arrive at qualitative judgments about his author's achievement and to define the value of this author for readers of all ages.

But why these four authors in particular? Why Brautigan, Vonnegut, Hesse, and Tolkien? Early in his book, *Future Shock*, Alvin Toffler asserts that "Writers have a harder and harder time keeping up with reality."* And, of course, it is possible that the "reality" captured by these four writers will soon cease to hold the attention of read-

---

* New York: Bantam Books, 1971, p. 5.

ers, that each of the four will soon be seen as someone who had a certain vogue in the late-1960s and early-1970s and then faded off the bookstore racks and out of the minds of readers. This is possible, but not, I think, probable. Despite the vagaries of taste and popularity, the strange chemistry that makes today's best seller next year's remainder item, it seems likely that all four authors focused upon in the Writers for the Seventies series will continue to hold the attention of American readers, particularly younger readers of high school and college ages.

Needless to say, the four authors are very different: Hesse, the pacifist, deep in Eastern religions and Jungian psychology; Tolkien, the Oxford don, absorbed in medieval literature and philology; Vonnegut, the former PR man turned satirist of an increasingly dehumanized America; Brautigan, that transitional figure between the Beat Generation and the Hippies, concerned with a gentle world of trout fishing and green growing things. Indeed, if we were to imagine the four of them in some Paradise of Authors (or—that favorite test-question situation—cast up together on a desert island), we might very well decide that they would have little to say to each other, about their works, about their interests.

Yet, for all their differences, there are some important common denominators running through the works of Hesse, Tolkien, Vonnegut, and Brautigan. Perhaps outlining a few of these will partly explain why all four writers began to attract large audiences in the United States at approximately the same time. First of all, speaking broadly, all four can be described as fantasy writers. Whether through interior fantasies (like *Steppenwolf* and *In Watermelon Sugar*) or through exterior fantasies (like *The Lord of the Rings* and *The Sirens of Titan*)—all four authors use fantasy to comment on re-

11

ality. Of course, any successful fantasy (from fairy tale to science fiction) comments in some way or other on ordinary reality. But our four authors have all, in their very different ways, been able to give their fantasies the sort of internal coherence, plausibility, and substance that enable their readers to suspend disbelief and accept what Coleridge called the "poetic truth" behind fantasy.

In common with that of virtually every significant writer of the last half-century, the reality behind their fantasies is pretty grim. In all four authors, a war—World War I or World War II—serves as either implicit or explicit background. The appalling catastrophe of the First World War, the slaughter of an entire generation of young men, seems always just beneath the surface of Hesse's major works; in Tolkien, the vast carnage of World War II paralleled exactly the composition of his own version of an ultimate struggle between forces of light and darkness; the Second World War has had the most direct influence on Vonnegut, who was in the war, a POW and a miraculous survivor of the hideous firebombing of Dresden; for Brautigan, the youngest of the four authors, World War II is coincident with his earliest conscious memories, and stands ironically as a time of coherence, when things were easier to understand than they could ever be again.

All four authors would surely agree with the "moral" of Vonnegut's *Mother Night:* "We are what we pretend to be, so we must be careful about what we pretend to be." In all four, this bare statement is developed in rich, complex terms. All four are ultimately concerned with self-definition, with the problem of a person's realizing his full humanity (or, in Tolkien's case, I suppose we must also say his full hobbithood). In all four, self-

12

fulfillment is threatened by an essentially dehumanized and dehumanizing world: Hesse's world of vulgar materialism, Tolkien's world in which Sauron aspires to enslave the spirits of all living creatures, Vonnegut's world in which machines often threaten to replace humanity, Brautigan's world of drop-outs from a society without sustaining values.

Finally—and perhaps the most important thing Hesse, Tolkien, Vonnegut, and Brautigan have in common—all four authors share an affirmative sense of the possibilities of the human spirit. Without denying the pitfalls that surround their characters, without settling for facile optimism, all four of these Writers for the Seventies show us in their works that there are still things a person can do, that there are still values to be found by looking around oneself and (even more important) by looking *within* oneself. In this time of disillusionment and danger, we need writers like Hesse, Tolkien, Vonnegut, and Brautigan—to remind us that joy is still possible, to teach us (in Hesse's phrase) how to hear the laughter of the Immortals.

Richard Brautigan is currently in the awkward position of having become something of a "cult hero" among the young, a real-life, larger-scale equivalent of the shy narrator of his novel, *The Abortion*, who becomes "a hero at Berkeley." The trouble with this role, of course, is that it becomes difficult to *see* the idol, surrounded as he inevitably is by admirers and detractors. It is always easier to measure an author's achievement when he's safely dead and buried and when we can discount the excesses of both his critical fans and foes, than when, as in Brautigan's case, the author is still young, still vigorous, still creating, still developing.

In this study, I have stressed (perhaps over-stressed) Brautigan's relationship to some of the major figures in American literature and to some of the central themes that run through this literature. I believe it is important to realize that although Brautigan is a highly original writer—there is no one very much like him, recent attempts to parody him have fallen flat—he is also directly in the native American grain. Brautigan is deeply aware of both today's America—the California that waits, he says, "like a metal-eating flower"—and of the mythic American past, that golden dawn of Lewis and Clark which he evokes so movingly in *Trout Fishing in America*.

The combination of Brautigan's feeling for the incongruities, absurdities, inhumanities of the present and his nostalgia for the lost past produces the curiously elegaic quality pervading much of Brautigan's best work. At the same time, the need—running through all his books—to seek a "good world" in the inhospitable American present gives Brautigan's work its surprising power.

Terence Malley
Long Island University
Brooklyn, New York

Contents

Preface.
Looking at Richard Brautigan

On the cover of the recent record album, *Listening to Richard Brautigan*, besides a picture of Brautigan and a very pretty girl and some brief, whimsical biographical information, is Brautigan's telephone number. In the picture, both Brautigan and the girl are holding telephones. The girl is smiling; Brautigan is holding out his phone, as if inviting communication. You can call him up any time you want.

The combination of telephones, telephone number,

and scanty biographical information indicates one of the most interesting paradoxes concerning Brautigan. On the one hand, there is the virtual exhibitionism implied by his reaching out for communication (and even more, of course, by his tendency to put his own picture—always accompanied by a young woman—on the covers of his books, as well as on the record jacket). On the other hand, there is Brautigan's well-known shyness, which has caused him to avoid interviews and has resulted in a relative paucity of biographical information about him. The supposed "interview" in David Meltzer's recent book, *The San Francisco Poets,* consists of a one-page statement by Brautigan on the relationship between his poetry and his novels. Perhaps the closest thing to a genuine Brautigan interview appears in Bruce Cook's *The Beat Generation,* but it too is very brief, with Brautigan agreeing to answer a few questions ("But only a few") and then suddenly and hastily fleeing.[1]

So, if you get Brautigan's record (Harvest/ST-424), you can call him up, provided you don't call late at night. (As he says, on *Listening to Richard Brautigan,* he never answers the phone after midnight, feeling certain it will be bad news[2]). But it's unlikely he'll tell you much about himself.

Similarly, Brautigan's books are for the most part both directly autobiographical and curiously elusive. For one thing, it's usually difficult to separate confession from whimsy in Brautigan's writing. For another, although he draws heavily on his pre-San Francisco experiences in his writing, those "old bygone days" are what he describes as "years and years of a different life to which I can never return nor want to and seems almost to have occurred to another body somehow

18

vaguely in my shape and recognition" *(Revenge of the Lawn,* 25).

Although nearly all of Brautigan's stories, novels, and poems are presented through a first-person narrator who is either similar or identical to the author, sometimes—as in such stories as "The Wild Birds of Heaven" and "Greyhound Tragedy," both from *Revenge of the Lawn*—he writes with the detached anonymity of a third-person narrative voice. Occasionally, too, Brautigan seeks separation of his fictional narrator from himself by referring to someone named "Richard Brautigan." This is an unusual but not unique device. For instance, two hundred years ago Tobias Smollett introduced himself as a character in his epistolary novel, *The Expedition of Humphry Clinker;* forty-five years ago William Faulkner presented a small dark man named "Faulkner" in his early novel, *Mosquitoes.* In Brautigan's *The Abortion,* among the regular contributors to the library for losers presided over by the narrator is one Richard Brautigan. "The author was tall and blonde and had a long yellow mustache that gave him an anachronistic appearance. He looked as if he would be more at home in another era" (28).[3]

This description of Brautigan evokes the various pictures of him on the covers of his books. Aside from his somewhat anachronistic appearance, there are nine important things (more or less) to keep in mind about Brautigan. 1) He's old enough (born 1935) to remember World War II, which provides numerous images and details in his work. 2) He was born and grew up in the Pacific Northwest—born in Tacoma, but lived in Oregon and Montana as well as Washington. 3) As everyone who's read *Trout Fishing in America* knows, he had an early and pretty thorough education in fishing, hunting, and general woodlore (not the least important thing Brautigan has in common with Ernest Hemingway). 4) He grew up in relative poverty; again, his awareness of his early life during the tag-end of the Depression contributes importantly to Brautigan's work. 5) He didn't go to college, though he has been poet-in-residence at Cal Tech. 6) He did go to San Francisco (in 1958), arriving there just in time for the Beat Generation explosion. "But my involvement with that was only on the very edge and only after the Beat thing had died down."[4] 7) He has lived in San Francisco ever since and is young enough to have been affected by the Hippie scene in the 1960s. (Thus, as many people have noted, Brautigan spans the gap between the Beat Generation and the Love Generation.) 8) For all his reticence, Brautigan obviously knows a lot of significant San Francisco writers, is at home in the West Coast literary scene; he has dedicated books to such fellow writers as Michael McClure, Don Allen, Jack Spicer, and Don Carpenter. 9) For what it's worth, he is an Aquarius (30 January); so am I.

Unlike such directly autobiographical American authors as Whitman, Henry Miller, Thomas Wolfe, and Jack Kerouac, Brautigan's experiences are seldom as important as his perceptions of these experiences. Like Lee Mellon in *A Confederate General from Big Sur*, Brautigan has "a wonderful sense of distortion" (82), through which even the most mundane events and memories are filtered.

In this book I'll be chiefly concerned with how Brautigan's imagination works, with how his "sense of distortion" shapes his and our world. In general, people who write or talk about Brautigan tend to be either snidely patronizing or vacuously adoring. Most of his reviewers damn him with the faint praise of words like "sweet" and "gentle"; many of the students I've discussed Brautigan with say he's groovy and let it go at that. I think that both of these responses are unfair to Brautigan's work. I'll try to take a good steady look at Brautigan's books, without either condescension or adulation, and to show what he's trying to say and how he's trying to say it. I believe that, like any artist's work, Brautigan's books can stand (and benefit from) critical scrutiny. And let me say right off that I believe Brautigan to be a genuine creative artist, if an uneven one. He is surely one of the most original writers of our time; at his best, and when he wants to be, he is also among the funniest. I believe that at least two or three of his books will have, as they say, a permanent place in American literature.

In trying to avoid both snide condescension and uncritical gee-whiz enthusiasm, one inevitably runs the risk of falling into the sort of solemn academic pedantry that murders the books one is dissecting. I'll try to avoid that. I admire literary critics like Leslie Fiedler, Robert Penn Warren, and (sometimes) Lionel Trilling, in whose essays you can feel a real passion for the books they're discussing.

My discussion of Brautigan's books will not follow the order of their publication. There's relatively little correlation between publication dates and composition dates. *Trout Fishing in America,* for example, was published in 1967, but, according to Brautigan, it was completed in 1961.[5] *In Watermelon Sugar,* published in 1968, was supposedly written during the spring and summer of 1964. *The Pill Versus the Springhill Mine Disaster* collects poems written over a twelve year period;

Revenge of the Lawn, stories and sketches spanning nine years. And so forth.

Instead I have organized my discussion from what I consider the lesser to the more significant books. I begin with a very brief survey of Brautigan's poetry and then a somewhat more detailed examination of his recent collection of stories, *Revenge of the Lawn.* Although there may be some merit to the argument that Brautigan is better "over short stretches,"[6] in short stories, poems, single episodes, than in whole novels, I think that most of the best "short stretches" occur in the novels. Since like most writers Brautigan comes back to or hovers around recurrent themes, a preliminary survey of his shorter works provides a kind of introduction for a more detailed look at his longer works. Moving on to the novels, I go from *The Abortion* (which seems to me to be the least successful of the four novels) to *A Confederate General from Big Sur* to *In Watermelon Sugar* to *Trout Fishing in America* (the most famous and most acclaimed of the four). This sequence not only follows what seems to be the general order of popularity of these books—among both critics and general readers—but also (I hope) it enables me to make logical transitions from book to book. At the end I have a concluding chapter in which I try to pull things together and to make some generalizations and judgments about Brautigan. Since this book is intended for the general reader interested in Brautigan's work, I have limited my discussion to the seven books of his that are now readily available; as far as I know, it is just about impossible to get hold of a copy of *Lay the Marble Tea,* for instance.

I have probably indulged in too much plot-summary. I hope that this won't be tedious for readers who have read all of Brautigan's books. I wanted people who haven't read them all to be able to get some sense of what the books are like (though Brautigan doesn't plot-summarize very easily) and to be able to follow my discussions. As any critic must, I would hope that readers of this book will be stimulated to turn (or return) to Brautigan's works, to look at Richard Brautigan on their own. As Brautigan says, "Hey! This Is What It's All About!"[7]

Chapter One.
Magic Up and Down:
The Pill Versus the Springhill Mine Disaster and *Rommel Drives on Deep into Egypt*

Near the end of his brief remarks on the relationship between his poetry and his novels—almost as an after-thought—Brautigan says, "I tried to write poetry that would get at some of the hard things in my life that needed talking about...."[1] I suppose that most poets agree that this is where lyric poetry comes from: the need to clarify and communicate one's inner feelings, or "the hard things" in one's life. From Brautigan's statement we might expect his poetry in general to be

24

intense, personal, confessional, private. However, though the images in many of his poems are very private indeed, sometimes even to the point of unintelligibility, for the most part his poems are more exterior than interior, more observations of the world around him than revelations of his inner feelings. Speaking very broadly, the nearly 200 poems that make up *The Pill Versus the Springhill Mine Disaster* and *Rommel Drives Deep into Egypt* can be divided into three general categories: personal poems; poems of fantasy or whimsy, often with a strong surrealistic quality; poems of observation and social comment.

The personal poems, including a sizable group of love poems, are more prominent in the earlier volume, *The Pill*. This book was dedicated to a Canadian girl named Marcia Pacaud, and about a dozen of the poems in it are or seem to be addressed to her. Among what we might call the Marcia poems are "Horse Child Breakfast," "The Beautiful Poem," "The Shenevertakesherwatchoff Poem," "Map Shower," "I've Never Had It Done So Gently," "Your Necklace Is Leaking," "I Lie Here in a Strange Girl's Apartment," "I Live in the Twentieth Century," "Nine Things," "Gee, You're So Beautiful That It's Starting to Rain," and "The Garlic Meat Lady from." These poems range from lyrical tributes to laments, and from them emerges what Brautigan calls "the legend/of her beauty" ("Garlic Meat Lady," 106), a portrait of a young woman who is not only beautiful, gentle, and passionate, but also in perfect harmony with the elemental rhythms of life. Thus, the Marcia of the poems can be compared to such serene heroines of Brautigan's fiction as Elizabeth, in *A Confederate General from Big Sur*, and Pauline, in *In Watermelon Sugar*. In "The Shenevertakesherwatchoff Poem," Marcia's habit of always wearing "a clock/strapped to your body" becomes symbolic of her representing the "correct time" (7). In "The Garlic Meat Lady from," Marcia's thorough caressing of the meat with garlic cloves fills Brautigan with a sense of the rich possibilities of life. This is essentially the overall significance of Marcia in these poems; she endows any action or gesture with a sense of glory. Her hair is described as a map that makes all places beautiful ("Map Shower," 29); her necklace diffuses a beautiful "blue light" ("Your Necklace Is Leaking," 42). And this radiance transfers itself to the speaker of the poems who, in "The Beautiful Poem," looks down at his own penis "affectionately" after twice making love to her (4).

The joyful self-esteem to be derived from a good love relationship is an important element in these poems, for, as in most of his fiction, the speaker of many of Brautigan's poems is readily susceptible to self-doubts, depression, or defeat. In one of the poems in *The Pill*, Brautigan expresses the depression of the rejected lover, vividly if somewhat inscrutably, by comparing himself to "a sewing machine/that's just finished sewing/a turd to a garbage can lid" ("I Feel Horrible. She Doesn't," 49).[2]

Although Brautigan sometimes strikes a genuine lyrical note in his poems celebrating a happy love relationship (besides such effective poems as "The Garlic Meat Lady from" and "Map Shower," in *Rommel Drives* "We Stopped at Perfect Days," "Deer Tracks," "Color as Beginning," and "As the Bruises Fade, the Lightning Aches," all seem to me successful lyrics), sometimes his "up" love poems tend to be somewhat gushy, overdone (e.g., "I've Never Had It Done So Gently Before" and "Your Catfish Friend," from *The Pill*.) Similarly, his "down" poems frequently run the risk of collapsing into mere self-pity. Hostile critics like to pounce on the mawkish little poem "Please" (from *Rommel Drives*)— which Jonathan Yardley has aptly described as having the worst qualities of a Hallmark greeting card poem—[3] as typical of Brautigan's poetry. Taking a poet's worst— and it would be hard to top (or bottom?) "Please" for that dubious position among Brautigan's poems—for his typical is obviously unfair, but it must be admitted that there are times when he is unable to get beyond sentimentality or bathos (e.g., "I Live in the Twentieth Century," and "Automatic Anthole," from *The Pill*; "30 Cents, Two Transfers, Love," and "The Moon Versus Us Ever Sleeping Together Again," from *Rommel Drives*).

But often Brautigan brings a poem to life with wit or humor. One of my favorite poems in *The Pill* is "My Nose Is Growing Old." In a way, this poem can be considered a contrast to "The Beautiful Poem." Instead of the speaker expressing affection for his penis as a result of a happy love affair, he singles out quite another appendage as the scapegoat for his anticipated lack of romantic success. All would be well if not for that inch or so of nose that shows its thirty-one years: "the rest/ of the nose is comparatively/young" (67). Then, from wondering if girls will still find a man with an aging nose desirable, the speaker leaps to the conclusion that they won't and imagines "the heartless bitches" gossiping about his poor old nose. This poem works, I think, because of the witty irony of the speaker rationalizing his anticipated failure with women and then literally finding his own explanation as plain as the nose on his face, thereby setting up what is in effect a self-fulfilling prophecy.

Brautigan's tendency to go from a conjecture to an

27

assumption (in "My Nose Is Growing Old," from "I wonder" to "I can hear them now") is related to his characteristic device of going from a simile (like) to a literal condition (is). It is one of the most unusual and interesting aspects of all of his writing, and sometimes it makes for strange, effective poems. In "Sonnet" (which is not a formal sonnet, needless to say, just as the several haiku poems in *The Pill* are not formal haiku), Brautigan attempts to convey an impression about the sea by comparing the sea to an old nature poet (perhaps Wordsworth, that staunch defender of the sonnet form?) who died of a heart attack in a public toilet. By the middle of the poem, it's as if Brautigan had forgotten the beginning term of his simile (the sea), as he goes on to describe the ghost of the dead poet haunting the toilet in his bare feet. The poem ends, "Somebody stole/his shoes" *(The Pill,* 74). Here, we can follow the progression of the figurative language (sea like poet; poet dead of heart attack in public toilet; poet still haunting toilet in bare feet; someone stole poet's shoes), and, if the poem works (which I think it does), the ending sends us all the way back to the beginning of the poem to ask, 1) Why "Sonnet"? and 2) What's the sea got to do with anything? The thirteen-line non-sonnet form contributes directly by paralleling the non-fulfillment of our expectations (i.e., about the sea and why it's like a dead nature poet). The sea is certainly not like the sea of a John Mansfield poem or a hearty sea-chanty. Instead, it is forlorn, scarcely able to make its ghostly and barefooted presence felt. But it is there, hauntingly, perhaps on the edge of our consciousness (like those seedy old men who hung around the public rest rooms of everyone's childhood). In short, I believe this poem communicates a valid and evocative

28

impression of the sea and at the same time implicitly and wittily comments on our stereotyped expectations of how the sea will be described.

In my view, Brautigan is not always this successful in developing a far-fetched image, simile, or metaphor. Sometimes the problem is that the central image (or the relationship between the two terms in a simile or metaphor) remains inaccessible. We can't really get at the meaning of the title symbol of "Horse Child Breakfast" or "The Pomegranate Circus" (from *The Pill*). In such poems as "The Fever Monument," "A Boat," "The Wheel," and "Poker Star" (all from *The Pill*), we can't follow the development of the imagery and put the poem together. Occasionally, as in "Shellfish" (from *Rommel Drives*), the poem itself seems to cohere (we can follow the movement from penny to dollar to wounded eagle to the sky), but the title itself is baffling.

From idiosyncratic or even arbitrary details and symbols, it's only a short leap to fantasy or surrealistic poems. Some of Brautigan's poems have a curious, dreamlike quality that might remind a reader of Bob Dylan's early dream-songs or that brilliant sustained surrealistic vision, *Tarantula*. In one poem, "The Symbol" (from *The Pill*), Brautigan even focuses on the same mythic figure that Dylan briefly employs in his "115th Dream," Moby Dick. For both poets, the great unconquerable enigmatic white whale of Melville's novel has become a comically diminished thing: for Dylan, the whale winds up as the wife of a deputy sheriff; for Brautigan, as a truck-driver delivering a load of seagulls, who praises union-boss Jimmy Hoffa. The fantastic extravagance of "The Symbol" is typical of Brautigan. We might possibly expect to find Ishmael or Captain Ahab transformed into truck-drivers; by using Moby Dick himself, Brautigan shows us even more emphatically just how anachronistic the old man-against-the-sea theme has become. This sort of satiric commentary on cherished literary myths runs all through Brautigan's work: one of the stories in *Revenge of the Lawn* is a compressed reworking of Jack London's *The Sea Wolf* which indicates how preposterously dated the 1904 novel seems sixty-five years later ("A Short Story about Contemporary Life in California"); throughout *A Confederate General from Big Sur* Brautigan parodies aspects of the myth of the American Dream; *Trout Fishing in America*, of course, may be approached as a satiric elegy to the vanished or vanishing great outdoors.

The use of fantasy in satiric commentary is also important in the nine-part poem, "The Galilee Hitch-Hiker" (from *The Pill*), which I believe to be one of Brautigan's finest achievements. The different parts of this poem are unified by Brautigan's depiction of Baudelaire as the central figure throughout. But the Baudelaire of Brautigan's imagination is scarcely the sinister *poète-maudit* of literary history and biography, scarcely the tormented author of *Fleurs de Mal.* (Indeed, the similarity between the names of the two poets might even lead one to suspect a whimsical identification between Baudelaire and Brautigan himself.)

In the various parts of "The Galilee Hitch-Hiker," we see Baudelaire giving Christ a lift to Golgotha in his Model-A; Christ is headed for a carnival concession, but Baudelaire proclaims his destination to be "anywhere/out of this world!" (52). (Again, incidentally, we might be reminded of Bob Dylan—here the Dylan of those strange, cryptic parables on the *John Wesley Harding* album, such as "The Ballad of Frankie Lee and Judas Priest.") We then see Baudelaire in San Francisco's skid row, commending an ageless wino for his drunkenness. He next appears dancing like an organ-grinder's monkey for a little boy who pretends his mother's coffee grinder is a hurdy-gurdy. In the fourth —and funniest—part of the poem, Baudelaire opens a hamburger stand but serves his indignant customers "flowerburgers/instead"(55). In the following two parts, we see Baudelaire as a magician—conjuring up "a twenty-one/jewel Siamese/cat"(56) and transforming an ordinary room into first a painting by Salvador Dali and then one by Van Gogh. Part Seven finds Baudelaire at his ease at a baseball game, equipped with a hot dog and an opium pipe; an angel commits suicide, the infield cracks like a mirror, the game is called "on/account of/fear" (58). Next, Baudelaire poses as a psychiatrist and takes over an insane asylum, and when he leaves, the insane asylum follows him around "like a strange cat" (59). Finally, in a return to the nostalgic mood of Part Three, Baudelaire participates in a child's funerals for insects and tiny birds, contributing "little prayers/the size of/dead birds"(60).

The parts of "The Galilee Hitch-Hiker" range from comic to sinister in mood, but throughout Baudelaire is a figure who is "out of this world." The first (and title) section of the poem sets up a contrast between Christ, who accepts martyrdom (though seeing his crucifixion as a mere carnival side-show), and Baudelaire, who will rattle on in his old Model-A, not stopping at Golgotha. At the risk of sounding a bit pretentious, I'll say that for Brautigan his Baudelaire figure symbolizes the creative imagination, which can transform an ordinary room into a masterpiece of art, and which can likewise trans-from the dull toyless life of a poor child in a slum-dwelling into the exotic (to a child) career of an organ-

31

grinder. Baudelaire is the "old/cloud merchant"(57) who feeds us flowerburgers instead of hamburgers and who urges us, as much as the old wino, to "always be drunk"(53). He is the artist who can transform anything into anything else, who can even transform our madhouse world into a cat purring against his leg.

In my view, Brautigan's sense of the transforming power of art (of the imagination or the heightened perception) is at the root of one of his chief strengths as a writer—and is also responsible for the unevenness of his work, especially of his poetry. As I've said, the distinction between *like* and *is* tends to blur in Brautigan's poems. Lost ships and doomed generals as a bouquet of flowers ("General Custer Versus the Titanic"), a plate of ice cream as Franz Kafka's hat ("Kafka's Hat"), vultures as race horses ("Horse Race"), taking a birth control pill as precipitating a mining disaster ("The Pill Versus the Springhill Mine Disaster")—all from *The Pill*; sheep as pennies ("Sheep"), an infant as a brain-surgeon ("The Sister Cities")—from *Rommel Drives* . . . wildly incongruous analogies are transmuted into identities to striking effect. Anything, as Baudelaire shows us, can be anything else. But sometimes, as Brautigan says in "After Halloween Slump," his "magic is down"(*The Pill*, 101), and the juxtaposition of seemingly incongruous terms either seems forced or remains inscrutable.

And sometimes, too, no real transmutation takes place, and the poem remains inert. For another important aspect of Brautigan's notion of poetry seems to be that virtually anything he (or anyone else?) writes down is a poem. This, in fact, is just what he asserts in "April 7, 1969," where he follows a flat statement of depression by saying he wants to write a poem: "any poem, this/

poem" (*Rommel Drives*, 54). Similarly, in "Albion Breakfast," the statement that a girl has asked him to write a poem *is* the poem (*The Pill*, 77), while in "All Girls Should Have a Poem" the commendable sentiment of the title is more or less the poem itself (*Rommel Drives*, 40).

Perhaps everything or anything is a poem, but surely merely to say, "Gee, I'd like to write a poem," or even, "Hurrah, I've just written a poem," is to wind up with, at best, a pretty lame poem. Bruce Cook praises Brautigan's "Critical Can-Opener" (*Rommel Drives*, 10) as a devastatingly witty-put-down of the New Critics, presumably for their over-insistence on detailed examination of the poem as a tight verbal structure.[4] But to the question posed by Brautigan in "Critical Can-Opener"—can we find what's wrong with this poem?—we can counter with regard to a fairly large number of his poems by asking what's right with them.

Especially in the more recent (and probably less selective) *Rommel Drives* volume, all too often there just isn't very much verbal "magic" to Brautigan's poems, and all we wind up with is a concise statement or observation. Of course, if everything is a poem, then the words in a poem aren't all that important anyway. Indeed, perhaps you can even have a poem without any words. And, as a matter of fact, in *Rommel Drives* Brautigan does have four "poems" that consist only of a title followed by a blank page ("A 48-Year-Old Burglar from San Diego," "1891-1944," "8 Millimeter (mm)," and " '88' Poems").[5]

Obviously the words in a poem do matter. About the best that can be said for Brautigan's blank poems is that they have brevity. (Of course—and this may be Brautigan's intention—there's plenty of space on the pages of these blank poems if you want to write in your own poem under Brautigan's title, a bit like those records where you're supposed to play or sing along with a professional musician or singer, or like a fill-in-the-dots picture, minus the dots.) Brautigan is much better off, surely, when he's striving "to name/the objects of this world" ("Private Eye Lettuce," *The Pill*, 5), when, as poets have always done, he's trying to bring something alive for us with his words or showing us how to see something in a new way.

Some of Brautigan's best poems, in my opinion, have a quality of fresh, precise observation. At times Brautigan reminds me a bit of William Carlos Williams. I assume that this is no coincidence and that Williams is a poet Brautigan admires. Significantly, in *A Confederate General from Big Sur*, a young man who derides Dr. Williams is promptly buried by a small landslide. After being dug out, the narrator tells us, "the next day he began reading [Williams'] *Journey to Love* rather feverishly"(62). For all his penchant for extravagance of image and for fantasy, Brautigan is like Williams in that he obviously also delights in the mundane, in the ordinary, in the sudden small illumination. Like Williams, too, he is able to give life and vitality to the most ordinary sight or occurrence. He makes a good poem out of a businessman staring at the unattractive rear-end ("like/a moldy refrigerator"!) of an unpretty girl ("Mating Saliva," *The Pill*, 92) and of the strange, quiet serenity of "The Winos on Potrero Hill," who "could almost/be exotic flowers"(*The Pill*, 15). In poems like these (and others, such as "The Widow's Lament" and "In a Cafe"—both from *The Pill*), Brautigan is transforming his observations, not merely recording them.

Based on what Brautigan says or implies about his

poems in the poems themselves, we might infer that Brautigan's attitude toward his poetry—toward all poetry —is somewhat ambivalent. On the one hand, there is the feeling that the poet is a kind of magician, capable of transforming anything into anything else, able to provide sudden insights or flashes of illumination for his readers. This is the attitude behind many of Brautigan's best poems, I think, whether fantastic extravaganzas like "The Galilee Hitch-Hiker" or small, cryptic, imagistic poems like "The Vampire" (*Rommel Drives*). It is, of course, an ancient conception of poetry, going back to the times when poets really *were* considered magicians. It is an attitude that was held by such earlier poets as Blake and Yeats, and is held by many contemporary poets, such as Allen Ginsberg and Brautigan's friend, Michael McClure.[6]

But not only is Brautigan's magic down sometimes; it often appears as though Brautigan doesn't really believe in the magic of poetry at all. In what is to me one of his most unattractive poems, Brautigan begins with the unpromising image of a piece of green pepper falling off a wooden salad bowl, and then asks, "so what?" ("Haiku Ambulance," *The Pill*, 43). So what, indeed. Often, in poems like this, the mockery seems to be mainly self-directed. Or, as in the poem titles followed by blank pages, there's a self-conscious put-on quality. By implying that writing a poem is all a game or a put-on, the poet sort of protects himself from hostile criticism. At times in his poems and even in some of his short stories, Brautigan seems fairly close to John Lennon's view that art is all a con-game anyway and that anyone who looks into a song or a poem or a painting is making a fool of himself. According to Lennon, all artists just "stick things in" to fake out their audience.

35

"I bet Picasso sticks things in. I bet he's been laughing his balls off for the last eighty years."[7]

Brautigan's ambivalence toward poetry—toward art— runs, as I've suggested, all through his work. It comes up importantly in relation to literature in general in both *The Abortion* and *In Watermelon Sugar*. In a story called "Homage to the San Francisco YMCA" (*Revenge of the Lawn*), he explicitly mocks the idea of taking poetry too seriously. The story deals with a lover of "good verse" who goes to the fantastic extent of replacing his plumbing with his favorite poets—including John Donne, Shakespeare, Emily Dickinson, Vladimir Mayakovsky, and (inevitably) Michael McClure. The man is soon driven nearly crazy by his lyrical plumbing fixtures, quickly learns that poetry just can't replace plumbing, and, after he's been kicked out of his own house by Mayakovsky and McClure, he winds up living happily ever after at the San Francisco YMCA, a place with good plumbing and, God knows, no poetry.

As is clear from Bruce Cook's brief interview with Brautigan, Brautigan is not only shy, he's also modest. He is very anxious that Cook not make him out to be an important member of any literary coterie and that Cook not draw "any big literary point" out of his habit (similar to Jack Kerouac's Spontaneous Prose) of typing out his works as fast as he can, 100 words a minute on an electric typewriter.[7] Similarly, and rather mysteriously, Brautigan insists that he only began writing poetry to learn how to write sentences so that he could write novels.[8]

The unevenness of Brautigan's poetry, then, can perhaps be at least partly explained by his self-conscious doubts about his poems, about poetry. In a sense, one might even say that the bad poems—thin or flat, hollow

36

or wooden, banal or inert—serve as a kind of protective screen for the good, the genuine poems. As long as Jonathan Yardley, say, is going after sitting ducks like "Please," he won't be looking into the richer and more interesting poems. It would be a mistake, I think, to try to elevate Brautigan much above his own self-evaluation that he is "a minor poet" (*Revenge of the Lawn*, 128). But I believe that at his best—in perhaps two dozen or so of the poems in *The Pill* and *Rommel Drives*—Brautigan is a true poet, a poet of originality, wit, imagination, and insight. In his best poems, Brautigan can make his readers feel like that friend of his who came over to read one of his poems, returned later to reread it, and then said, "It makes me want to write poetry" ("Hey! This Is What It's All About!" *The Pill*, 66).

Chapter Two.
All the Small Victories:
Revenge of the Lawn

In discussing Brautigan's most recent book, *Revenge of the Lawn* (1971), one encounters some of the same problems as in trying to give a coherent account of his poems. Although certain motifs recur—nostalgia, loneliness, an identification with losers, a feeling for nature, an awareness of the limits of communication, a sense of the incongruities of American life—the stories, sketches, parables, anecdotes, mood pieces, impressions, observations that make up *Revenge of the Lawn* are very miscellaneous and therefore hard to generalize about. One thing to be said right off is that in this book Brautigan shows a lot more variety than he's usually given credit for. *Revenge of the Lawn* can't quite be called "a complete history of America"—Brautigan's phrase for the smells of a small-town auction ("The Auction," 123) —but it does include not only a wide range of subjects and settings but also of tones and even of styles.

About the only thing all sixty-two stories have in common is brevity; the longest piece in *Revenge of the Lawn* is less than seven pages, while the shortest runs only three *lines*. In fact, another thing to be said here is that Brautigan can write with real economy. It is surprising to come back to some of the stories in *Revenge of the Lawn* for a second reading and discover that they're only two or three pages long; one remembers so many details, so much happening—all in a few pages.

As in his poems, Brautigan is pretty uneven in *Revenge of the Lawn*. Some of the stories are full of compressed energy, power, insight; others, as Anatole Broyard has said, "never get beyond easy vignettes, light enough to blow off the page."[1] On the whole, however, I think that Brautigan is more successful in these short prose pieces than in his poems. And I think that this greater success comes chiefly from Brautigan's narrative ability, from his gift for bringing even the slightest, most inconsequential, most unpromising situation to meaningful life.

Brautigan's story-telling gift can be seen in the very first tale in *Revenge of the Lawn*, the title story. "Revenge of the Lawn" moves along by means of non-sequitor and calculated digression. In structure, it is somewhat similar to Mark Twain's "The Story of the Old Ram," that comic masterpiece of narrative indirection. Where Twain puts his story in the form of a hope-lessly rambling monologue by old Jim Blaine, who "always maundered off, interminably, from one thing to another, till his whisky got the best of him, and he fell asleep,"[2] "Revenge of the Lawn" consists of a loosely organized autobiographical memoir about Brautigan's grandmother, a Washington State bootlegger of "grand operatic" proportions (9). However, unlike "The Story of the Old Ram," "Revenge of the Lawn" does have a coherent theme—and a very important one for all of Brautigan's work.

After an opening description of the grandmother, Brautigan moves on to an imaginary and rather trivial conversation between her and the local sheriff, in which a certain "Jack" is mentioned. We soon learn that Jack is a man who had arrived at the grandmother's house to sell vacant lots in Florida and had stayed for thirty years. It is Jack, we are later told, who "let the lawn go to hell"(12).

But meanwhile Brautigan meanders along to explain how Jack had come to replace his grandfather. The grandfather, it seems, had been "a minor Washington mystic"(11), who had predicted the exact date of the beginning of World War I. But the burden of prophecy had been too much for him and he had gone insane, living out the rest of his life in an asylum, believing himself to be a small boy waiting for a chocolate cake his mother was baking (see the cover of *Revenge of the Lawn*). "It took seventeen years for that chocolate cake to be baked"(11).

By this point in the story we're pretty far away from the bootlegging career of Brautigan's grandmother, of course. But Brautigan has more or less sidled into an important contrast between his grandfather and Jack.

The grandfather was very short, and "He had a dark idea that being so short, so close to the earth and his lawn would help him to prophesy the exact date when World War I would start"(11). Jack, although he arrived "selling a vision of eternal oranges and sunshine" (10), takes an instant aversion to the lawn in front of the grandmother's house; he believes the lawn is "against him"(10).

When the story circles back to Jack again, we learn further that Jack believes, with some reason, that *all* nature is against him. Not only does the yard (i.e., the former lawn) contrive to stick nails in the tires of Jack's car or sink the car itself in mud, but also bees—drawn by the pear tree in the yard—delight in stinging Jack in "the most ingenious ways"(12). And, in the climactic episode of the story, a flock of geese (which had been plucked by the grandmother, after they all got drunk on some mash and passed out, which (of course) caused the grandmother to assume instantly that they were all dead . . .) appear before Jack in the yard like ghastly apparitions—or, as Brautigan says, "like some helpless, primitive American advertisement for aspirin . . ."(14). This rattles Jack so badly that he drives his car "into the house for the second and last time in the Twentieth Century"(14); the other time was when a bee had run along Jack's cigar to sting him on the lip.

"Revenge of the Lawn" ends with a kind of postscript or coda, separated by asterisks from the main text, in which Brautigan's autobiographical narrator enters the story directly. He relates what he calls his "first memory of life": Jack cutting down the pear tree (co-conspirator with the lawn, the bees, and the geese), pouring kerosene on it, and then setting fire to it, "while the fruit was still green on the branches"(14). I'm not sure that

41

this postscript was thematically necessary. From the title, the depiction of Jack as the enemy of nature, and the contrast between Jack and the grandfather (between the man who tries to deny the power of nature and the man who is overwhelmed by its power), the point of Brautigan's tale is clear, for all his digressive technique. But the coda is important in emphasizing a major theme in all of Brautigan's work—the self-destructive madness of abusing nature. (This theme is also worked out comically in "A Need for Gardens" (69-70), in which some men persist insanely in trying to bury a live lion in a hole in the ground that is much too small, indignantly rejecting the narrator's suggestion that they plant some carrots instead.) It's worth remembering that the small boy who watched Jack burn the pear tree grew up to write *Please Plant This Book*, in which Brautigan says,

The only hope we have is our
children and seeds we give them
and the gardens we plant together ("Lettuce").

If "Revenge of the Lawn" is an important story thematically, it is also, in my view, one of Brautigan's funniest pieces. Part of the humor comes from the digressive structure of the story, from the way Brautigan circles around that former lawn with its pear tree and bees. Also, as often in Brautigan, there are some fine comic details; the whole treatment of the episode in which the geese get into the mash and have a fine time until they all pass out—"They looked as if they had been machine-gunned" (13)—is handled with wonderful comic energy and economy. Perhaps most important of all in the success of this story is the way Brautigan manages to sustain a very effective deadpan tone throughout "Revenge of the Lawn." This quality (which, by the way, comes through very well on the record, *Listening to Richard*

Brautigan) is also reminiscent of Mark Twain. In his essay, "How to Tell a Story," Twain defined what he considered the essentially American "humorous" story; his definition pertains to many of his own stories (e.g., the famous "Celebrated Jumping Frog of Calaveras County"), and it pertains to "Revenge of the Lawn": "The humorous story is told gravely; the teller does his best to conceal the fact that he even dimly suspects that there is anything funny about it. . . ."[3]

My brief discussion of "Revenge of the Lawn" has been, I see, more than half as long as that story itself, a good example of what I meant before by Brautigan's narrative economy. But, at just under six pages, "Revenge of the Lawn" is, in fact, one of the longest pieces in the volume. Some of the stories in *Revenge of the Lawn* are even more compressed. "The Wild Birds of Heaven," which runs about four pages, is interesting not only as an example of Brautigan's narrative economy, but also because it is quite unlike what one might think of (with some justice) as a "typical" Brautigan story. All four of Brautigan's novels and almost all of the sixty-two stories that make up *Revenge of the Lawn* are first-person narratives with at least some degree of identification between author and narrator. Even when the narrator is not a central character (as in "Revenge of the Lawn") or even when the narrator is clearly a fictional persona and not "Richard Brautigan" (as in *The Abortion*), the voice behind the story obviously speaks for the author; we accept the narrator's view of things and receive his judgments as the author's. But in "The Wild Birds of Heaven" (there are a few other stories in this category, most notably "Greyhound Tragedy") Brautigan keeps himself—his personality and his judgments— out of the story entirely, and writes a traditional third-person narrative. Traditional but nevertheless very strange.

The story concerns a harried, middle-aged, middle-class white-collar worker named Henly, who is faced with a rebellion in his household. He arrives home from work one day to receive an ultimatum from his three children: either he buys them a new television set or they become rampant juvenile delinquents. His wife chips in with "Get a new television set for the kids. What are you: some kind of human monster?"(52). Since we're told that this is "the kindest thing" she's said to her husband in years, we have a pretty clear immediate idea of their relationship. Mr. Henly agrees instantly to his children's demand and goes off to a large department store where he picks out a huge, expensive TV set. He wants to buy the set on credit, and he's sure that his credit will be good because, as he explains, he's "already 25,000 dollars in debt"(53).

Up to this point the story reads like just another version of that overworked "Bringing Up Father" motif in American culture. But strange things begin to happen. Mr. Henly's credit-interview is with an amazingly beautiful young woman, who looks to him "like a composite of all the beautiful girls you see in all the cigarette advertisements and on television"(52–3). Her effect on Mr. Henly is to immediately make him light up a cigarette. She approves his credit and sends him through a wondrous door with a doorknob of pure silver.

Mr. Henly finds himself in, of all places, a blacksmith's shop, where he is instructed to remove his shoes and socks. Then, after he is measured, Mr. Henly's shadow is removed by the blacksmith, who replaces it with "the shadow of an immense bird"(54). Mr. Henly is told that he will get his regular shadow back when he finishes his time payments for the TV set. On his way out, he again passes the beautiful girl in the credit department, again reaches for a cigarette, and is mortified to discover that he has smoked his last one.

What Brautigan is saying in this small fable—again with great economy and, I think, with considerable power—is that Mr. Henly is indeed "some kind of human monster," as his wife calls him. The details are very important in "The Wild Birds of Heaven," and they work together beautifully. We're told at the very beginning of the story that Mr. Henly's job in the insurance company he works for is to keep "the dead separated from the living"(51) in different filing cabinets; near the end, the blacksmith goes to another filing cabinet, where he keeps different bird-shadows. The enigmatic bird-shadow that Mr. Henly has tacked on to his feet is a kind of albatross replacing Mr. Henly's own shadow; it makes visible what has already happened: the extinction of any real identity for Mr. Henly.

Mr. Henly is the affluent consumer reduced to nothing but his role as buyer. Taking away his shadow is an ironic act because he himself is nothing but a shadow. He responds reflexively to all commands to buy; as I've said, he reacts to the beautiful girl in the credit office as if she were literally a compelling advertisement for cigarettes. When he runs out of cigarettes, at the end, he earns the girl's contempt, just as, we may be sure, when he runs out of credit he will earn increased contempt and enmity from his own family. When he exhausts his credit, Mr. Henly will exist only in the file cabinet of his own insurance company (the cabinet reserved for the dead) and in a comparable file cabinet in the blacksmith's shop where, presumably, his shadow will be placed. In terms of the folk song quotation that

45

Brautigan begins his story with, the file cabinet is the only "dark holler" [hollow] that waits for Mr. Henly. The title, another quotation from the song, is also ironic; the shadow of the bird that is affixed to Mr. Henly's feet by the blacksmith who waits behind the fabulous gaudy door is anything but a wild heavenly thing. Mr. Henly will remain in the tame hell of middle-class credit-buying, at least until his credit runs out. After that, he has only the file cabinet marked "dead" to look forward to.

As I've said, "The Wild Birds of Heaven" achieves its effect indirectly. Brautigan does not comment on his tale or tell us how to respond. Nevertheless, the point comes through clearly and powerfully. In another story, "The Betrayed Kingdom," Brautigan goes to the opposite extreme and explicitly points up the message. This kind of direct moralizing is fairly common in Brautigan's poems, but not in his stories; many readers will question, I think, whether Brautigan's comment at the end of "The Betrayed Kingdom" is really necessary.

The story is actually little more than an anecdote about a girl who worked a sort of sexual con game to induce men to drive her home from parties. But it is skillfully and swiftly told, and (with or without the author's direct final comment) it is an important story thematically. Also—one of the most interesting aspects of the story—"The Betrayed Kingdom" is told with a bitterness that is unusual in Brautigan's writing. This quality is clear right from the beginning, from Brautigan's heavily sarcastic description of his story as a "love story." Later, he uses sarcasm again in reference to the setting in which the story takes place: "Oh, those Beat Generation days! talking, wine, and jazz!"(140).

The girl the story centers on is a kind of ironic Cinderella-figure. She comes to parties "all sexied up" (139) and drinks wine and comes on strong until, always promptly at midnight, she declares that she has to go home and asks whether any man will give her a ride to Berkeley. Lured by her implicit sexual promises, some unsuspecting man always offers her a ride. Each time, the man winds up sleeping alone and cold on her floor, for "Miss Berkeley Floor," as the narrator calls her, doesn't sleep with anyone. Finally, she gets her come-uppance, of a sort. Having drunk too much wine one night, she vomits on the front fender of the car of one of her victims. When the girl pulls her usual sleep-on-the-floor trick on him, he is so angry that he leaves her vomit on his car (presumably the evidence that she's only human after all and shouldn't be so high and mighty) for everyone to see, until it wears off months later.

In this story, the autobiographical narrator is more an observer than a participant. He doesn't have a car and he knows about the girl's trick anyway, so he isn't one of "the stung"(141). And yet, as I've said, his tone is unusually bitter and sarcastic. The reason for this bitterness becomes clear when he comments at the very end of his account that "This might have been a funny story if it weren't for the fact that people need a little loving and, God, sometimes it's sad all the shit they have to go through to find some"(141). Although "The Betrayed Kingdom" of the title refers literally to the girl's vomit "residing" on her victim's car, we might say that a more important sense of that phrase would refer to the sad betrayal of the kingdom of human relations by the girl's cynical practices.

Quite a few of the stories in *Revenge of the Lawn* are informed by Brautigan's sense of "all the shit" people

47

have to go through to find some loving. It is a major theme in Brautigan's work. In "Coffee," for instance, the narrator begins a day by dropping in on a girl he'd formerly been close to and receives only a grudging cup of instant coffee for his efforts to revive the relationship. Much later, after a long day of meaningless talk and joyless drinking, he drops in on another girl in a similar effort to revive an old relationship. But, once again, they have nothing to say to each other; he asks for a cup of coffee, which he does not want, and is left alone in the kitchen, while the girl goes back to bed, to fix himself another cup of instant coffee. Here (and in stories like "Pacific Radio Fire" and "April in God-Damn") I think that Brautigan is successful in dramatizing the painful frustrations of not being able to either accept one's loneliness or do anything about it. The man whose wife has just left him in "Pacific Radio Fire" can't think of anything to do but set fire to his portable radio while it plays Top-40 love songs, and the narrator is keenly aware that there's nothing he can do to help his friend, that "words can't help at all"(29).

As I've said, this theme of the painful difficulty of establishing and maintaining an emotional relationship runs through all of Brautigan's work. With different emphases, it is a major element in three of his four novels— *The Abortion, A Confederate General from Big Sur,* and *In Watermelon Sugar.* A reviewer of the *Revenge of the Lawn,* Josephine Hendin, has even asserted that it is *the* major theme in Brautigan and gives a kind of unity to the miscellaneous stories in *Revenge of the Lawn.* As Miss Hendin sees it, "Brautigan makes cutting out your heart the only way to endure. . . . Brautigan people live with no passionate attachment to anyone or any place and never permit themselves to feel a thing."[4] Although I think Miss Hendin's view is exaggerated and somewhat simplistic—in many stories the need for attachment is stronger than the impulse toward non-attachment; in others the desire for non-involvement is not realized—on the whole her point has considerable validity. At the very least, her view is a useful corrective to those critics and reviewers who seem to regard Brautigan as an amiable but addled front man for the Love Generation.[5]

One of the slightest sketches in *Revenge of the Lawn* is called "Ernest Hemingway's Typist." There's next-to-nothing to it; it's only about a page long, an amusing little meditation on the thrill of knowing someone who's had some typing done for him (at fifteen dollars an hour) by the woman who used to type Hemingway's manuscripts. Brautigan begins this sketch by saying that the phrase itself, "Ernest Hemingway's Typist," sounds like "religious music"(60). Even though Brautigan is writing with tongue in cheek here (among other things, this magical typist produces "paragraphs that look like Greek temples"(61)), it might be said that there is a serious point to his tribute to Hemingway's typist.

I believe that, along with Mark Twain, Ernest Hemingway is one of the deepest influences on Brautigan's writing. This influence is obvious enough in relation to Brautigan's feeling for nature, as seen in the many fishing stories in *Revenge of the Lawn* as well as throughout *Trout Fishing in America*. But I think that the relationship between Brautigan and Hemingway goes further than that, and can also be seen in the subdued tone of some of Brautigan's stories. Like Hemingway, Brautigan frequently works for emotional effect by understating his feelings or by not stating them at all. As in many of Hemingway's earlier short stories, Brautigan frequently

49

uses the point of view of an adolescent in *Revenge of the Lawn*. In general, these stories concern the young man's feelings of separateness, isolation, alienation. Although it can be argued that "A Short History of Oregon" suffers once again from the final comment tacked on by the author,[6] otherwise that story is a good example of what might be called Brautigan's Hemingway manner.

"A Short History of Oregon" is a brief autobiographical account of an afternoon's hunting in an Oregon forest. The narrator is sixteen and is not primarily interested in shooting a deer, but rather in feeling "the awareness of hunting"(106). As he makes his way through the trees, he comes upon a ramshackle house "right there in the middle of my private nowhere"(106). He is somewhat displeased by this intrusion of the outside world into his solitude. As he passes the house, four children appear, one after the other, to stare at him silently from the porch of the house. He passes the children silently. Not a word is exchanged. The story ends, "I had no reason to believe that there was anything more to life than this"(107).

As I've said, it's questionable whether this intrusive final sentence really contributes to "A Short History of Oregon." Even without it, we have the sense of a lonely teenage boy assuaging his loneliness by making it absolute. The sudden reminder of an outside world disturbs him, and, of course, the run-down house ("more of a large shack than anything else" (106) is itself a metaphor for his loneliness. So are the four strange children, with nothing to say to each other or to him, as he passes, with nothing to say to them.

"Forgiven" is another story that might remind one of Hemingway. The story has a strange framework. For some reason (perhaps only as a little joke) Brautigan has written "Forgiven" as if it were not by "Richard Brautigan"; the story begins and ends with apologies to Richard Brautigan for invading his literary province, for writing "something in the same theme" (manner?) as *Trout Fishing in America* (165). But in its dominant mood "Forgiven" is actually quite unlike most of the episodes in *Trout Fishing in America*.

Like "A Short History of Oregon," "Forgiven" is an autobiographical narrative concerning a lonely teenage boy who goes into the wilderness seeking utter solitude as a remedy for the relative solitude of his life. Here, rather than "the awareness of hunting," the narrator is after the serenity of fishing. On a rainy afternoon he hitchhikes to the Long Tom River (also mentioned in the story "Elmira"), which he describes as "the beginning answers to some very complicated questions in my life . . ." (165), and he begins to fish.

His usual procedure in fishing the Long Tom is to move downstream from one bridge to another, a half mile away. "It was gentle fishing between the bridges, down through a lazy dripping landscape" (166). But on this day the fishing is poor and so he moves further down the river, away from the bridges where the fishing is gentle. He moves into an area of six "big swampy pools" (167). These pools, reminiscent of the dark swampy place that the protagonist of Hemingway's "Big Two Hearted River" fears and avoids, draw the narrator on until, suddenly, when he reaches the sixth pool, night falls and he is overcome by a strange panic. "Every horror in the world was at my back . . ." (167), he says, and he quickly returns to the safety of the bridges.

It would seem that the narrator has gone too far in. Enjoying the solitude of his fishing, he is finally overcome by that solitude. Then he has to get out; he has to

51

return from the utter solitude of the pools to the bridges, which serve as symbols of human presence. By understating the emotional state of his teenage narrator, Brautigan gets a lot of power from his presentation of the ambiguous solitude that comes from escaping society and going into the wilderness; the experience is something to be pursued, but not too far. The other side of the serenity of nature is its terror.

In "1/3, 1/3, 1/3," Brautigan gives us a rather different story of lonely adolescence. Here, the loneliness of the narrator is shared, as he becomes the "1/3" partner in a hopeless literary project. Near the beginning of the story, the narrator describes himself as a "lonely and strange" seventeen-year-old living in a cardboard-lined shack in a run-down area of a town in the Pacific Northwest (19). Across the muddy unpaved street from his shack lives the second "1/3" in the dubious partnership that develops, a tiny divorced woman in her late thirties who exists, along with her young son, on the bullying charity of the Welfare Department. She forges the alliance and introduces the narrator to the final "1/3" of the triumvirate.

As she explains her plan to the narrator, we learn that she knows a man who is writing a novel. Since this would-be author has only a fourth-grade education, the woman is to edit the novel, to fix up the spelling and grammar. She has "read a lot of pocketbooks and the *Reader's Digest*"(21). The narrator's role will be to type the edited novel; the woman knows he has a typewriter because she has heard him tapping away late at night. The partners will share equally in the proceeds of the novel: 1/3 each.

At the beginning of the story, the narrator has nothing more to do with his life than watch the dark sky and eat an apple, so he readily agrees to the woman's scheme. They go to the run-down trailer the novelist lives in, where the narrator meets a man in his late forties who looks "as if life had given him an endless stream of two-timing girlfriends, five-day drunks and cars with bad transmissions"(20). The bargain is sealed and at last the narrator gets to see the manuscript on which all their hopes depend.

A friend of mine who teaches at the University of Washington believes that everyone over forty in the Pacific Northwest has written a novel; I think he feels that it has something to do with the influence of the lumber industry on the collective imagination. The book by the novelist in "1/3, 1/3, 1/3" is in fact about lumbering, and, alas, it must be about as bad as any of the novels misbegotten by all that wood. The story ends with the narrator reading this illiterate and utterly banal manuscript—the adventures of a noble logger in love with a virtuous waitress—while rain falls steadily on the trailer, while the three partners are "all sitting there . . . pounding at the gates of American literature"(24).

This seems to me to be one of the most successful stories in *Revenge of the Lawn.* The partnership of these three lost souls is deftly and plausibly handled. And Brautigan manages to get both humor and pathos out of his story. Some of the details are very funny (such as the bedraggled half-dog, half-cat creature that sits on the steps of the novelist's trailer, going "Arfeow!"), but the overall effect of the story is to illuminate the sad, impossible dream of artistic glory and wealth that makes people respond to "You Can Draw" matchbooks or makes them answer ads for "Famous Writers School." The narrator is once again the lonely aimless adolescent, but as he reads the hopeless manuscript (transcribed, appropriately, in a Hopalong Cassidy schoolboy's notebook) perhaps he comes to realize that he doesn't yet know the meaning of aimlessness or loneliness.

Except for "The Betrayed Kingdom" (which takes place in the late 1950s), all of the autobiographical stories I have discussed so far have been set either in the period of adolescence or in the very recent past. However, there is a third large group of stories in *Revenge of the Lawn* going all the way back to Brautigan's childhood, a period corresponding more or less to the years of World War II. Miss Hendin finds in these stories the seeds of what she calls Brautigan's "quirky peace of the supercool," and argues that the daunted and defeated child of such stories as "Corporal" and "The Armored Car" was father to the "lonely and strange" adolescent and grandfather to the adult who flees deep attachments.[7]

Maybe so. But to me the general tendency of Brautigan's childhood stories is more in contrast to themes that run through the adolescent and adult stories than it is parallel. Like many Americans who were born in the thirties, Brautigan seems to have considerable nostalgia for the World War II era. And with his fine eye for details he's very good at bringing this nostalgia out.[8] In part, his childhood stories can almost be considered a child-eye's equivalent of Richard Lingeman's fine book, *Don't You Know There's a War On?* Like Lingeman, Brautigan obviously enjoys rolling off World War II names, such as "Grumman Wildcat," and slogans like "Remember Pearl Harbor!"

The most important thing about childhood for Brautigan, it would seem, is that, paradoxically, it was a time when things were easier to fathom and cope with than they'd ever be again, a time before the really "complicated questions" began. Growing up during World War II, one took it for granted that everything mysterious (and there's much wonder and mystery in Brautigan's childhood stories) could somehow be related to the war effort. Thus, in "A Complete History of Germany and Japan," the narrator becomes accustomed to the horrible human-sounding death-shrieks of the pigs in the slaughterhouse next door by assuming that their screams "had something to do with winning the war. I guess that was because everything else did"(122).

Exposed to the constant stream of patriotic rhetoric that accompanies any major war, the child lives in a world that seems easy to comprehend. As the narrator of "Corporal" says, if enough children collected scrap paper, "we could win the war and destroy evil forever"(119). With the adults acting "as if they knew what was happening" ("The Ghost Children of Tacoma," 73), it was easy for the children to pick up the mood and vicariously do their part. Since to any American child the war was both far away and omnipresent, the child could participate imaginatively (e.g., the staggering totals of imaginary planes, ships, tanks, etc., racked up by the narrator of "The Ghost Children") without having the security of his everyday world threatened. Because of the coincidence of childhood and war, it could almost be said that for someone like Brautigan World War II could be called *the last good time this country ever had* (the ironic phrase used by the narrator of *A Confederate General from Big Star* to describe the American Civil War, 147).[9]

Even in the childhood stories that aren't specifically related to the war, this same sense of childhood as a time when one could cope with and understand his world comes through. "1692 Cotton Mather Newsreel"

55

is a story that balances the infinite mystery of childhood against the child's ability to cope with or control life's mysteries. The narrator depicts himself as an adventurous child resembling a "midget Don Quixote"(16), ready to accept any dare or challenge. He views his childhood as a time when "doors had a large meaning to them" (15), when, that is to say, answers lay waiting behind the mysteries of closed doors.[10] The specific mystery in "1692 Cotton Mather Newsreel" concerns a woman the neighborhood children have decided is a witch.

The narrator is challenged by his friend to go up into the "witch's" house and wave out the window. To live up to his reputation as a fearless boy, he takes up the dare and crosses the street to the house the woman lives in. As he makes his way toward her attic apartment, he examines her garbage and finds it just ordinary, not "witch garbage" at all. Her apartment itself yields nothing more sinister than vases and jars of flowers in every room. The woman is not at home and so the narrator is able to stand at her window and wave to his astonished friend.

After completing his mission, the boy is suddenly overcome by terror, and he runs screaming down the stairs and through the streets, with his friend, also screaming, running along with him. The dare has been met and conquered, but the woman's quite ordinary and slightly sad apartment has, with all of the flowers in every room, enough witch-evidence to maintain the pleasurable fantasy.

Like several of the other stories I've discussed, "1692 Cotton Mather Newsreel" includes a short comment tacked on to the end: "This was a month or two before the German army marched into Poland"(18). Broyard dismisses this ending as "a sententious bit of irrelevance."[11] But I think it does add to the story. I think that Brautigan is saying that with the coming of World War II, the very quality of childhood mystery and fantasy was to be changed—from traditional fantasies of speculation about the wicked witch living in a flowering attic to the kind of innocent but chilling fantasies of mayhem recorded in "The Ghost Children of Tacoma."

The significant thing about a story like "1692 Cotton Mather Newsreel" is the way the child manages to cope with his fantasy but still retain it. What for an adult would have been sufficient proof that the woman in the attic was no witch is for the child opposite evidence. The key factor in this story, as in many of Brautigan's childhood stories, is the power of the child's imagination to reshape reality. As I said in discussing Brautigan's poems, in "The Galilee Hitch-Hiker" a small boy living in a slum is able to compensate for his lack of toys and games by imagining himself an organ-grinder, churning hurdy-gurdy tunes out of his mother's coffee-grinder.

In "The Armored Car," the child is similarly capable of pretending that he delivers his morning newspapers in a huge armored car. In my opinion, the point of this tale is not, as Miss Hendin suggests, to show a lonely child taking refuge in a mobile fortress,[12] but rather to contrast the satisfying childhood world of imaginative fantasy to the adult world of disappointed expectations. "The Armored Car" begins with a brief account of the narrator winning a fountain pen by answering a one-question telephone quiz. The pen, he tells us, never arrived. Brautigan comes back to this seemingly unrelated episode at the end of his story by saying that the armored car of his childhood fantasy "was the only thing I ever won"(127).

In Brautigan's view, it would seem that childhood

ends when the imperatives of reality replace the fantasies of imagination. Thus, the fantasy campaign of dogfights, bombing, and strafing in "The Ghost Children of Tacoma" is infinitely more satisfying than a "real" campaign, the paper-collecting drive in "Corporal." In "The Ghost Children," the narrator chooses his own rank, since he's participating in his own fantasy campaign; he is a captain. In "Corporal," of course, despite his visions of becoming a general, the narrator is only able to accumulate enough scrap paper to make the lowly rank of corporal.

At the end of "Corporal," the narrator tells us that he gave up the frustrating unequal competition for old magazines and newspapers and "entered the disenchanted paper shadows of America where failure is a bounced check or a bad report card or a letter ending a love affair and all the words that hurt people when they read them"(120). This passage, I believe, comes as near as any in *Revenge of the Lawn* to the center of the book. Indeed, this theme of sympathetic identification with losers—the unsuccessful, the alienated, the odd—is right at the center of all of Brautigan's writing.

We have already met this general theme in several of the stories I've discussed: in the narrator's mute sympathy for his lonely friend ("Pacific Radio Fire"); in the narrator's adult identification with the woman whom children called a witch ("I look about as crazy in 1967 as you did in 1939," says the narrator ["1692 Cotton Mather Newsreel," 15]); in the implicit or explicit compassion for the victimized in such stories as "The Wild Birds of Heaven," "The Betrayed Kingdom," and "1/3, 1/3, 1/3." It is a theme that recurs throughout Brautigan's novels, perhaps most importantly in *The Abortion*, where the library presided over by the narrator is a focal point of unsuccess, a real "library for losers." It is also an important theme in relation to the surprising frequency of old people—superseded, unwanted, with nothing to look forward to—in Brautigan's books. In one story in *Revenge of the Lawn,* the narrator gets on a San Francisco bus, becomes uncomfortably aware that he is the only passenger aboard under sixty, and feels like a cruel trespasser. He says, "I felt terrible to remind them of their lost youth, their passage through slender years in such a cruel and unusual manner" ("The Old Bus," 72). Tactfully, he leaves the bus, though he's miles from his destination.

I suppose it could be argued that sometimes Brautigan risks mere sentimentality in his stories about losers. On the whole, however, I believe that this theme is responsible for some of his most effective stories. For one thing, in his short stories (unlike in the poems) Brautigan's sympathy or pity is rarely directed to himself, rarely becomes self-pity.

Two of the best tales in *Revenge of the Lawn,* "The Post Offices of Eastern Oregon" and "The World War I Los Angeles Airplane," are very much stories of losers. In "The Post Offices of Eastern Oregon" (the longest piece in the book at almost seven pages), Brautigan presents various losers. First and most important, there is the narrator's Uncle Jarv. At the beginning of the story, the narrator and his uncle are driving to a small town in Oregon where Jarv grew up. Jarv had been a local football hero and later "a legendary honky-tonker"(91), but now he has settled into a paunchy middle-age of Western novels, radio opera, and Copenhagen snuff. Because of his honky-tonk past and his extensive knowledge of fishing and hunting, however, Jarv remains an obvious hero to his teenage nephew.

They arrive at their destination just in time to see a man unloading the bodies of two bear cubs he's just shot. Virtually everyone in town turns out to greet Jarv and/or to examine the bears. Indeed, the two actions get mingled in the narrator's mind, as he says, "I expected the bears to say hello"(92). After a while the narrator and his uncle go to a small restaurant for lunch and then over to the post office so that Jarv can send a postcard. Here the narrator sees for the first time the famous nude photograph of Marilyn Monroe that became such an important part of her Hollywood build-up.

When they return to the house where the bears had been unloaded, the narrator and his uncle find that the two bodies have disappeared. The boy listens as Jarv and his friends sit around talking about high school football during the Depression and making "jokes about how old and fat they had grown"(95), until, just before nightfall, the bears are found. Some practical joker has dressed them in human clothes and placed them in the front seat of a car.

Like many of the stories in *Revenge of the Lawn*, on first reading "The Post Offices of Eastern Oregon" might appear to be no more than an inconsequential anecdote. But I think it is considerably more. Once again, Brautigan has ended his story with a coda (detached from the main text by a row of asterisks, as in "Revenge of the Lawn"), and here I think the coda is important. The narrator, writing ten years or so after the events he's just related, discusses the recent death of Marilyn Monroe and says that her suicide has brought that day in Eastern Oregon back to him. The effect of the coda is to set up a kind of three level relationship involving Uncle Jarv, with his life in the past and with little to look forward to except a thickening middle and thinning hair; the young bears—slaughtered carelessly, even wantonly (it's significant that no one really wants or needs the bears as meat; the mayor of the town accepts them, but chiefly because he has special craving for bear meat); and Marilyn Monroe, "young and beautiful, as they say, with everything to live for" (96). The slow death of Jarv, the violent death of the cubs, the suicide of Marilyn Monroe.

In referring to a slot machine in the restaurant where he has lunch with his uncle, the narrator tells us that "the county was wide open"(94). I think that what Brautigan is trying to convey in "The Post Offices of Eastern Oregon" is a kind of parable of prodigality, concerned with the wastage of life. The nonhuman bears are ruthlessly destroyed; the love goddess (I don't know whether Brautigan was aware of it, but the caption on the famous nude photograph of Marilyn Monroe is "Miss Golden Dreams") is no less ruthlessly driven to suicide—a beautiful loser. The strange joke of dressing up the dead bears in human clothes is paralleled by the image of wrapping up Marilyn Monroe's body in "a dull blanket"(96); both "dressings" are grotesque, unnatural, perverted almost. Jarv is a survivor, but also a loser, with nothing in front of him and when you come right down to it not much behind either.

"The World War I Los Angeles Airplane," the last story in *Revenge of the Lawn*, is also one of the most recently published.[13] The story is one of Brautigan's best, I think, and it should serve as a sufficient rebuttal to any critics or readers who may feel that Brautigan is already written out. "Los Angeles Airplane" has an unusual structure; it is one of the most emphatic examples of Brautigan's apparent fondness for numbered lists. For the most part, the story takes the form of a list of items which are intended to serve as capsule biography of and elegy for the narrator's father-in-law. The father-in-law is depicted as a man who struggled after the elusive American Dream until "he didn't have any more life to use"(174), as a loser who suffered defeats and humiliations and whose life can be summed up in thirty-three short statements, one of them repeated twice.

As in "Pacific Radio Fire," in "Los Angeles Airplane" Brautigan's narrator is painfully aware of the limits of communication. He has no words to prepare his wife for her father's death or to soothe her. He tries to think of "the best way to tell her that her father was dead with the least amount of pain but you cannot camouflage death with words. Always at the end of the words somebody is dead"(170).

The one repeated detail in the story is important. Early in his catalogue, the narrator tells us that his father-in-law had been a pilot during World War I and that his plane had once been followed through the skies over France by a rainbow. He then goes on to relate the father-in-law's early successes in banking and ranching, his subsequent business failures during the Depression, his new start in California, his humiliating forced retirement at the early age of fifty-nine, his degrading job as a janitor in the school his own daughter attended ("his working as a janitor was a subject that was very seldom discussed at home," says the narrator, with powerful understatement (174)), his eventual dwindling away into quiet, secret alcoholism, his lonely death in front of the family television set during an afternoon TV program. Then, almost at the very end of the story, in the thirty-second item, Brautigan returns to the one detail in this man's life that a person can come back to with more than pity or helpless sympathy. "Once he had been followed by a rainbow across the skies of France . . ."(174).

All that remains to be added to this sad list summing up a man's life is the statement that must follow whatever camouflage one tries to cover the unalterable fact with. The last item of the thirty-three repeats the narrator's words to his wife: "Your father died this afternoon" (174). In this restrained elegy for a good man who, like most of us, had more than his share of bad luck and frustrations, I believe that Brautigan has indeed achieved what at the beginning of the story he suggests he is trying to do; he has shown what the father-in-law's death "means to all of us"(171).

I have discussed only about one-third of the sixty-two stories in *Revenge of the Lawn,* and some of that one-third very sketchily. As I flip through the table of contents of the book, I see numerous stories that I probably should have gone into—humorous fantasies like "Complicated Banking Problems" (which Mark Twain might have written if he'd been born, as Brautigan was, exactly one hundred years later), strange mood pieces like "Blackberry Motorist," which nobody but Brautigan could have written. But I think that I have touched on most of the main themes and devices that Brautigan employs in his short fiction, in all his fiction for that matter. As I said earlier, I pretty much agree with Broyard's contention that some of Brautigan's stories are nothing more than "easy vignettes." But I also think that there are quite a few deeply meaningful stories in *Revenge of the Lawn,* enough, in fact, to justify considering Brautigan a master of the short short story. Throughout the book, he handles his narratives with ease and economy. Although the stories are generally too brief to allow much character development—and anyway Brautigan has maintained that he's not much interested in "character delineation"[14] —he is almost always successful at evoking the mood he's after, and his sense of detail is usually just right. Even the slight stories are mostly successful within their limits. And, as Brautigan reminds us, "One must keep track of all the small victories" ("Coffee," 35).

In the very best of the stories in *Revenge of the Lawn* —I would include the title story, "1/3, 1/3, 1/3," "The Wild Birds of Heaven," "A Short History of Oregon," "The Post Offices of Eastern Oregon," "The World War I Los Angeles Airplane"—Brautigan offers us genuine and moving insight, offers in each of these stories what he calls (in "A High Building in Singapore") "a goofy illumination" (47).

Chapter Three.
A Hero of Our Time: *The Abortion*

About four years ago, when I first started reading Brautigan, I saw a magazine advertisement that began, "My name is Richard. I write books. Want one?" Then it went on to say that you could get one of Richard's books by sending a dollar to an address in San Francisco. The first time I saw this ad I thought maybe this Richard was Richard Brautigan. But I don't think it was. The name given at the bottom of the ad was, if I remember correctly, Richard Lebow. Before I got around to sending my dollar, the ad stopped running. Or perhaps my subscription to the magazine ran out.

Since then I've often wondered whatever happened to the Richard of that ad and his books. Perhaps he finally took them all down to the library depicted in another Richard's novel, *The Abortion* (1971). The narrator of Brautigan's novel is a librarian (though curator might be a more accurate term). But the library he works and lives in is not the usual kind of place where people come to browse, to read newspapers, to borrow books. "This is another kind of library" (20).

This library, in fact, is "the place where losers bring their books" (48–9), a place where the books are reverently placed on shelves by their authors, never to be read by anyone. Eventually the books are stored in a large dry cave in Northern California. The purpose of this strange library is to make the various authors—of books ranging from *Growing Flowers by Candlelight in Hotel Rooms* (written by a very old woman) to one on masturbation (by a sixteen-year-old boy, "a little sadder than he should have been for his age" [82]), and including one called *Moose*, by someone named Richard Brautigan ("Just another book")—all feel wanted, "and to gather pleasantly together the unwanted, the lyrical and haunted volumes of American writing" (96).

The origins of this library are very mysterious and seem to extend far back into the American past. Indeed, the background of the library sounds like something out of Thomas Pynchon: so vague, so shadowy, so suggestive. But, whereas in Pynchon's splendid novel, *The Crying of Lot 49*, the Tristero conspiracy is subversive and disruptive, in Brautigan's book, The American Forever, Etc. (the foundation behind the library) seems to exist simply and amiably to provide a place for the lonely and untalented to bring their "unwanted" books. "This library came into being because of an overwhelming need and desire for such a place" (22). All we learn about The American Forever, Etc., is that it keeps scrupulous records of all the unread books brought to the library (including perhaps some from seventeenth-century New Amsterdam); that it pays its employees irregularly and in irregular amounts—when it pays them at all; that it has moved its library steadily westward, more or less paralleling the settling of America, from New York to St. Louis to San Francisco; that it now houses its books in a sturdy brick building right across from a garage with the big word "GULF" in front of it. The library, that is to say, seems to be a kind of metaphor for the loneliness of American experience and for the need to communicate somehow—last stop, right across the street from the Gulf, from the void that separates losers from winners. "What a strange place this library is," says Vida, "but I guess it's the only place you can bring a book in the end" (83).

The narrator—Foster calls him "the Library Kid," otherwise he's unnamed—is one of the losers who first came into the library to deposit a book. We don't find out what his book is about ("Just another book"?), but we do learn that he inherited the job as librarian because his predecessor was afraid of children. We learn too that he's either the thirty-fifth or thirty-sixth librarian. The figure is perhaps arbitrary, but it's worth mentioning (even if the notion seems a bit far-out) that Brautigan's novel was written during LBJ's administration, the thirty-fifth or thirty-sixth president (depending on how many times you count Cleveland); this coincidence, it seems to me, might suggest that the library is a metaphor for

America itself, and that its sequence of timid, strange, insecure librarians are comic equivalents of American presidents.

The narrator has never had any formal librarian training, but he's extremely dedicated to his job. When *The Abortion* opens, we learn that he hasn't been outside the library in years—three years, as we find out later. He remains on duty at all times, twenty-four hours a day, just waiting for the gentle little front doorbell to signify the arrival of another book brought by another loser. Besides his dedication, though, as long as he stays in his library he is free from the uncertainties and anxieties of the world outside.· "It was all pretty complicated before I started working here" (54).

Almost as soon as Vida arrives at the library with *her* book, she recognizes the narrator as one of those "not at home in the world" (52). And she should know because, as she realizes, she's another, another misfit, another loser. Vida's book is about Vida's problem, and Vida's problem is "a fantastically full and developed body . . . that would have made the movie stars and beauty queens and showgirls bitterly ooze dead make-up in envy" (43).

Vida's body has a long history in American legend and wet-dream. Katrina Van Tassel was wearing it when she freaked out Ichabod Crane in "The Legend of Sleepy Hollow"; the hero of George Washington Harris' wonderful *Sut Lovingood* tales was driven to near-mayhem by Cecily Burns wearing Vida's body; Eula Varner completely disrupted the life of the ascetic school teacher Labove with the body, in William Faulkner's *The Hamlet*; later, in *The Town*, she extended her area of devastation, chiefly at the expense of the quixotic lawyer Gavin Stevens; Griselda, in Erskine Caldwell's *God's Little*

Acre, made Ty Ty Walden want to get down on his hands and lick something when she wore it. . . . This list could be extended. Some might even say that the body Vida wears killed Marilyn Monroe . . . . It's a body so beautiful, says the narrator, "that the advertising people would have made her into a national park if they would have gotten their hands on her" (43).

Every man—every *male* from about four-years-old on —wants to get his hands on Vida's body. Only, Vida feels, it's not her body at all. The mythic American piece of ass believes that she's been locked into someone else's body; she looks to the narrator "as if her body were a castle and a princess lived inside" (42). Her body was meant for her sister, perhaps, Vida thinks, while her sister wears *her* long, slim body.

Vida's name is obviously important. *Vida* means life (Latin=*vita*), but when the narrator asks her how she pronounces her name, Vida says "V-(eye)-da" rather than "V-(ee)-da." And the "V-(eye)-da" pronunciation suggests something of her painful sense of having been leered at, *eyed*—". . . the object, veneration and butt of at least a million dirty jokes" (45).

Vida is filled with the bitterness of unearned guilt, for her beauty, "like a creature unto itself, was quite ruthless in its own way" (133). A high school boy drank hydrochloric acid because she wouldn't date him; a man drove his car into a train while gawking at her and died in her arms, muttering "You're beautiful" (47); English teachers "fall like guillotines" when they see her coming (53). Then they fail her when she won't come across.

Our timid narrator is of course not exempt from Vida's wondrous power. But—half out of timidity, half out of self-consciousness—he holds back. He comforts her with a candy bar (virtually his only social grace is distributing candy bars to the "troubled or worried") and some Gallo sherry, and very soon—despite Vida's awkwardness (she describes her body as "this awkward machine" (56))—they wind up in his bed, in his little room at the back of the library. And Vida decides to stay with him, in the library, even though she has doubts about the place. "I don't know how to break this to you," she says, "but you've got a pretty far-out operation going on here. This library is a little on the whacky side" (49).

The cover of the Simon & Schuster edition of *The Abortion* obligingly informs us that "This novel is about the romantic possibilities of a public library in California." By the point we've now reached (roughly one-third of the way into the novel), the "romantic possibilities" of the cover blurb seem to have been fully realized: the shy recluse/loser has found love and wonder exploring the miraculous charms of the legendary piece of ass; the sex goddess herself seems to have become quickly reconciled to her "grotesque" body, quickly cured of her self-hatred. Only the novel is really just beginning.

Almost immediately we learn that Vida has become pregnant. "Gentle necessity" causes Vida and the narrator to agree upon an abortion. Our unworldly narrator leaves the library—for the first time in three years—and, after one false start when he neglects to bring any money, he manages to make his way to a phone booth, from which he gets in touch with Foster, his partner in the library enterprise.

As with the characters of Jesse and Lee in *A Confederate General from Big Sur*, in *The Abortion* Brautigan sets up a basic contrast between the narrator and Foster. The narrator, as I've said, is shy, introverted, passive, not at home in this world. Until Vida becomes pregnant, he is a virtual recluse, almost a hermit. It's quite appropriate that Vida should refer to "his" library as "the monastery" (208). Foster, on the other hand, is a wild caveman from the caves where the older library books are stored. He is loud, outgoing, a kind of buffalo of a man charging about in his eternal rain-or-shine, cold-or-hot-weather T-shirt. Having none of the narrator's reverence for the library, Foster wants to replace the softly tinkling bell at the front door with something louder. He refers to the library as an "asylum" (he means, of course, a lunatic asylum, a place to keep people *in;* the narrator would surely accept the word—he thinks of the library as an asylum too—but for him asylum means place of sanctuary, a place that keeps the world *out*). Foster is not even very conscientious about his end of the library operation; he horrifies the narrator by letting slip the fact that the books under his care are threatened by "cave seepage." Foster has all the worldliness the narrator lacks and he is easily able to arrange for a quick abortion in Tijuana ("THE MOST VISITED CITY IN THE WORLD" (159)).

Almost the entire last two-thirds of *The Abortion* deals with the preliminary arrangements for the trip down to Tijuana, the trip itself, the operation (which goes smoothly: ". . . no pain, all clean. The usual" (180)), and the trip back to San Francisco. The narrator and Vida return safe and sound from Tijuana, only to discover that in their absence a fierce woman has expelled Foster from the library and has taken over. To his distress—but to the glee of Foster and Vida—the narrator realizes that he will now "have to live like a normal human being" (223).

The book ends with the narrator, Vida, Foster, and a

girl from Pakistan all sharing a little house in Berkeley among the students. As predicted by Vida, the narrator has become "a hero" in Berkeley among the students. Despite his "new life" and his new status, however, the narrator has not quite broken with his old, library life. For he tells us, on the very last page of *The Abortion*, that he spends his days on the Berkeley campus gathering contributions for that mysterious library foundation, The American Forever, Etc.

The Abortion is Brautigan's longest novel so far, by a good deal, but it is also the one in which the least happens. The pace is very leisurely; for instance, the author devotes eleven pages to getting the narrator and Vida into bed together for the first time and then cuts out chastely on the (still preliminary) line, "*We kissed*" (68). This lack of fast-paced action—along with an accompanying lack of dramatic tension—is one of the most surprising and audacious things about *The Abortion*.

A timid librarian and a girl filled with self-hatred caused by her *Playboy* body meet, fall in love, decide immediately to have an abortion when the girl becomes pregnant, go and have the abortion, and, as far as the main plot goes, that's about all there is to it. We're not used to things working out so smoothly in books. In particular, in literature the course of abortions hardly ever does run smooth. They're much more likely to end in death and despair than in a slight fatigue and a great relief. In John Barth's *End of the Road* (1958), for example, the woman having the abortion suffocates horribly on her own vomit; in Faulkner's *The Wild Palms* (1939), the hero, an ex-internist, performs the abortion himself, fouls it up, and his lady dies from internal hemorrhaging. . . . So it seems to go in literature. In Brautigan's novel, however, Vida is in the capable hands of Dr. Garcia, and everything goes well: "The usual." A couple of hours after the operation, she is eating clam chowder at a sparkling Woolworth's in downtown Tijuana, and she is able to return to San Francisco the same day.

Brautigan's low-keyed, anti-dramatic, anti-heroic treatment of the trip to Mexico, the actual abortion, and the return to San Francisco is surely deliberate, even determined. In fact, in his description of the bus ride from San Diego to Tijuana, Brautigan shows indirectly the contrast between his *Abortion* and more usual literary handling of the subject. On that ride the narrator and Vida are seated behind another young American couple. The narrator infers that this couple are on a mission similar to the one that's drawing him and Vida to Tijuana. This other couple, however, appear to belong in another world—or at least in another story. They are grim and tense, and at one point the woman seems to be about ready to cry. "Those people in front of us," Vida says, "are worse than the idea of an abortion" (159). This other couple, indeed, could have stepped out of Hemingway's bleak abortion story, "Hills Like White Elephants," in which a young couple find themselves bitterly estranged—communication impossible, the relationship dead—by the idea of an impending abortion. We might even suspect that Brautigan had Hemingway's story in mind as a contrast to the main situation in *The Abortion*, for the last we see of this unhappy couple in Brautigan's novel they are disappearing into the Mexican equivalent, so to speak, of Hemingway's Spanish white hills: " . . . into some hazy yellow poor-looking hills with a great many houses on them" (160).

The low-keyed, almost uneventful quality of the abortion journey—of virtually the entire novel—is directly related to the role of the main character, the librarian-narrator, in *The Abortion*. He is unnamed in the novel, as I've said, and I believe his lack of a name is important (as it is also in *Trout Fishing in America* and (especially) *In Watermelon Sugar*) because it's one minor way of suggesting that he's nobody special. He's only a man, and a rather passive one at that. Nevertheless I think Brautigan means us to take seriously the narrator's later designation as a hero at Berkeley. In fact I believe Brautigan means us to accept his timid librarian as a "Hero of Our Time."

About 125 years before the time in which *The Abortion* is set, the Russian soldier and poet Mihail Lermontov published a novel called *A Hero of Our Time* (1840). Lermontov's hero, Pechorin, was a suave, dashing, somewhat swaggering figure—the antithesis of Brautigan's librarian. But the very incongruity of considering the narrator in *The Abortion* a "hero" seems to me to get near the heart of what Brautigan is suggesting in his novel.

The Abortion is subtitled "An Historical Romance 1966," and looking back those five years from its publication date we can see the justice of Brautigan's subtitle. Even with our short five years' perspective, we can already see 1966 as a time when some of the qualities exemplified by the narrator seemed to have a vitality and viability that now are lost or all-but-lost. In 1966 the general Peace and Love scene seemed to be growing and spreading from San Francisco to New York, and the sharks hadn't begun to move into Haight-Ashbury or the East Village in force yet. 1966 was a time, too, when the Beatles—as well as other people—still had it together

74

and were still mainly singing gentle songs. When Vida brings the narrator to her apartment, after he's been expelled from the library, virtually the first thing she does is to play the Beatles' *Rubber Soul* album for him. It's no coincidence that a whole series of Mexican cabdrivers identify the narrator as a Beatle. Although Brautigan underplays it (as he does almost everything in the book), it might be said that one whole dimension of *The Abortion* is a sad, nostalgic elegy for a set of conditions that already, only five years later, seem very long gone. Perhaps already some of the qualities of Brautigan's narrator seem as remote from us (only five years later) as the qualities of Pechorin in Lermontov's novel.

The same qualities that make the narrator an ideal employee of the library for losers make him this strange, passive, low-keyed hero of our time. He tells us at the very beginning of the book, "My clothes are not expensive but they are friendly and neat and my human presence is welcoming. People feel better when they look at me" (13). He welcomes the people who bring him their lonely lives and unwanted books, and he makes both their lives and books seem important, even if only for a while. (The books are never to be read, the people leave the library taking their loneliness with them.) He greets them ceremoniously with a smile, or even (in Vida's case) with a candy bar and sherry. His "training," as he sees it, is perfect for his library work. "I have an understanding of people and I love what I am doing" (23).

But—as a former Beatle, Ringo Starr, has recently expressed it—it don't come easy. The narrator's progress from library hermit to Hero at Berkeley is neither easy nor smooth. As I mentioned before, for him the library has been a kind of monastery or asylum, a fortress from the complexities of modern life. And he is reluctant to give up his fortress and "discover the Twentieth Century all over again" (121).

Before he and Vida decide to go to bed together he tells her a little of his pre-library life, concluding "It was all pretty complicated before I started working here" (54). He is obviously hesitant to become deeply involved with another human being, which is to say with life. Perhaps, in fact, this is why the narrator clings so determinedly—even fanatically—to the elaborate ceremonies of the library; ritualization is a kind of detachment; dealing with people's lonely unwanted books enables him to avoid having to really deal with their (or his) lonely unwanted lives. Even in the midst of his rather clumsy undressing of Vida, the narrator hesitates. "It would have been much simpler just to have kindly taken her book for the library and sent her on her way . . ." (63). He describes the process of undressing Vida as if it were a war. "Each garment was won in a strange war" (64). This is appropriate because every gesture of involvement is a struggle—inner as well as outer. When the narrator goes to call Foster for abortion advice (the first time he's left the library in three years), his struggle with the door of the phone booth is similar to his struggle with Vida's bra.

But he does get involved, despite his anxiety and passivity (it is *Vida* who suggests that they first go to bed together), and his involvement leads him from a completely passive role to a more active one. In planning the abortion arrangements, Vida and Foster do most of the talking. And Vida drives Foster's van to the airport, since the narrator can't drive. But as the journey goes on—especially after the operation, when Vida is weak and tired—the narrator becomes steadily more decisive. In the course of the novel as a whole the narrator learns—and it's surely one of the central themes of *The Abortion*—to go "fragile step by fragile step, until you've done the big difficult thing waiting at the end, no matter what it is" (109).

But it don't come easy. And neither, really (and despite the relative ease and efficiency—"the usual"—of the actual operation), does the abortion itself. The narrator describes the joint decision to have an abortion as "arrived at without bitterness and . . . calmly guided by gentle necessity" (71). Neither Vida nor the narrator feels mature enough to have a child yet; they both agree "An abortion is the only answer" (71). Once the decision is made they never hesitate or second-guess each other.

Yet even the smoothest abortion is a rather rough business. What the librarian calls "the surgical hands of Mexico" turn out to be quite efficient but also very unpleasant. If the United States is depicted in *The Abortion* as a lonely land full of people needing to communicate, if even vicariously (the unread books piling up in the caves), Mexico is the place where Americans go for divorces or abortions: "WELCOME TO TIJUANA THE MOST VISITED CITY IN THE WORLD" (159). Quite apart from the sordid make-a-buck hustle that pervades the Mexico portion of *The Abortion* (even the kindly and efficient Dr. Garcia tries to overcharge the narrator and Vida), Mexico is presented as a dangerous, even sinister place. Very early in the novel the narrator mentions that one of his predecessors in the library is planning to move to Mexico with a poet. He adds, "I believe it's a mistake on their part. I have seen too many couples who went to Mexico and then immediately broke up when they returned to America" (24). And of course during their short stay in Mexico the narrator and Vida are virtually surrounded (as well as depressed) by their fellow American *abortionistas*—the young couple on the bus who disappear into the hills, a high school girl and her furiously respectable parents, a grimly laconic couple. In the doctor's office, the narrator wonders, "What were we all doing there?" (173).

Moreover, on the trip down to Tijuana—mixed in with the sterility of San Francisco's airport, the sleaziness of San Diego ("There are too many unlaid sailors there . . . ," Vida says [106]), the sordidness of Tijuana itself —mixed in with these images of inhospitable cities, Brautigan places numerous images of life and fertility that seem to comment on or even to mock the abortion quest. Before they reach the San Francisco airport, the narrator looks out the window of Foster's van and sees "a sign with a chicken holding a gigantic egg" (128). Throughout their journey they encounter the color green, symbolic of new life and vitality; in San Diego they stay at the Green Hotel, which has a large green plant in the window; even Dr. Garcia's office building is painted green. It isn't until Vida and the narrator reach Tijuana that we realize that the abortion journey takes place in the spring, the season of rebirth, for the narrator mentions that the local Woolworth's has as its window display "Easter stuff; lots and lots of bunnies and yellow chicks bursting happily out of huge eggs" (165).

Brautigan's description of the actual abortion is about the most dramatic and—to my mind—the most effective episode in the whole book, though as usual the drama is underplayed. As I've said earlier, due partly to our conditioning by literature we don't expect an abortion to go smoothly in fiction. We're expecting the worst, and so, of course, is the narrator. While the operation takes place, the narrator sits in another room, waiting, helpless, listening to the conversation of the doctor and his very young assistants, to the clink of surgical instruments, most of all perhaps to the periods of "noisy silence" (179). The whole scene is done with a Hemingway-like restraint, by means of which the narrator's fear and helplessness come through very powerfully, as he sits there in the dark, waiting.

I'm not suggesting by all the above that Brautigan's *Abortion* should be regarded as an anti-abortion tract. Neither before nor after the operation do the narrator and Vida repent their decision. (Vida's final comment is "You're looking at the future biggest fan the Pill ever had" [200].) But Brautigan is not as simple (or simple-minded) as some of his condescending critics believe. "Gentle necessity" is a stern taskmaster; even a "perfect . . . No pain, all clean" (188) abortion don't come easy.

Vida's literal abortion has a strange parallel in the narrator's final expulsion from his library asylum. When the narrator learns that the fierce woman has taken over the library he goes through a kind of internal convulsion. "My heart," he says, "and my stomach started doing funny things in my body" (221–2). He has become, as it were, the unwanted fetus expelled from the snug library womb.

Actually, though, the process is more like a premature birth in which he's somewhat untimely ripped—before he feels ready to give up the library—than like an abortion. It's necessary for the narrator to come out of his monastery and to continue coping with life, as it was necessary for Vida to come out of the prison castle of her body. But (again, Brautigan is not simple-minded) part of the narrator continues to cling to the comfortable womb of the library. As I've said, even at the end of *The*

Abortion the narrator tells us he's a kind of small scale fund-raiser for the foundation that supposedly keeps the library running.

The foundation, again, is called "The American Forever, Etc." The initials suggest a possible anagram: FATE. I mention this possibility because throughout *The Abortion* Brautigan has numerous references to fate or "gentle necessity." After resolving to have the abortion, the narrator says, "It was absolutely too late for remorse now or to cry against the Fates. We were firmly in the surgical hands of Mexico" (107). When he and Vida arrive in Tijuana and are searching for Dr. Garcia's office, the narrator says, "Fourth Street had waited eternally for us to come as we were destined to come . . ." (167). A few pages later, when they arrive at the doctor's office, the narrator tells us, "the door to the doctor's office opened effortlessly as if it had always planned to open at that time . . ." (171). Upon returning safely to San Francisco, he feels like one who has completed a predestined journey: "It felt very good to be in the van after having travelled the story of California" (219).

I think that the various references to fate are related to what I have called the Hero of Our Time motif in the book. When the narrator and Vida are in San Diego, the desk clerk of the Green Hotel tells them, "People should never change. They should always be the same" (202). We might think the narrator would agree with this idea, for he himself tends to resist change. But he does not agree; in fact it's only out of politeness that he is able to "hold a straight face" (202).

The point is that the narrator—and perhaps the characters in Brautigan's world in general—is caught up in a world of change: call it fate or gentle necessity. A world he never made and one which he has little control over. He may wish to stay in the relatively eventless, choiceless, changeless library. And he may even harbor a nostalgia for it after he's been expelled. But coming out he retains his humanity and he copes as well as he can. No adventurer, he nevertheless proceeds along "fragile step by fragile step . . ." (109).

Recently a half-dozen brief parodies of various contemporary American authors appeared in *The New York Times'* Sunday Book Review section.[1] Being parodied is obviously a measure of fame, since there's no sense in mocking the mannerisms of an author unless you're certain your audience will be familiar with his work. The mere fact that Brautigan was one of the writers parodied in *The Times* indicates that his work has started to draw wide attention, beyond the limits of *Rolling Stone* and college bookstores. He's in prestigious company too; flanking the piece on Brautigan are parodies of Donald Barthelme and James Baldwin, both authors whose books inevitably receive serious critical attention.

The writer of *The Times'* parody of Brautigan is the novelist Walker Percy. He based his piece on *The Abortion,* calling it "The Mercy Killing: A Love Story, by Richard Brautigan." Walker Percy is a very talented writer, a winner of the National Book Award, but, in my opinion, his Brautigan parody is not very good. He seems to think that Brautigan takes a simple-minded delight in the idea of abortion in his novel; in his parody Percy has the two main characters cheerfully handing over the heroine's mother to a doctor for extermination. That's a pretty silly idea and, as I've tried to show, it really has nothing to do with what Brautigan is getting at in his novel.

81

The other important aspect of Percy's parody is the way he echoes and exaggerates Brautigan's stylistic mannerisms. Early in *The Abortion*, the narrator looks down at the sleeping Vida and says, "I could see one of her breasts. It was fantastic!" (17). Percy has his narrator say the same thing, almost verbatim, twice within a couple of hundred words. Brautigan's general tendency towards simple, direct, fairly short, somewhat repetitive sentences is exaggerated by Percy to a point of extreme monotony. And so on.

Actually I think Brautigan is a fairly difficult writer to parody successfully. First of all, he has more variety of tone and style than Percy seems to give him credit for. Brautigan's virtuosity of style is more evident in *Trout Fishing in America* than in *The Abortion*, but even in the latter there is a lot of difference between the way he writes when, for example, he describes the meeting between the narrator and the old woman who's written a book on growing flowers by candlelight, and the way he writes when describing the narrator's anxiety while he waits for the abortion to be performed. In the first scene, the tone is involved, quietly enthusiastic, warm; in the second, it is detached, restrained, almost numb. In one Brautigan sounds a little like William Saroyan; in the other, very like Hemingway.

Brautigan is a fair parodist himself; at times in his work, I believe, one can detect him mimicking, whether with reverence or derision, the styles of such American writers as Hemingway, Stephen Crane, Jack London, Jack Kerouac, and Kenneth Patchen. In *The Abortion*, as I've said, he appears to echo Hemingway both in his account of the young couple on the bus and in his depiction of the actual abortion. Parodying a parodist is obviously very difficult. Moreover, in all his writing,

Brautigan shows a fondness for the mundane characteristics of actual speech patterns, in their full repetitious banality. Perhaps the best example of this in *The Abortion* is when Brautigan repeats the sentence, "Purchase a cocktail" (215), six times in seven lines to indicate the "sing-song inhuman voice" of an airline stewardess. Again, Brautigan's occasional parroting of ordinary speech is hard to parody, since its very essence is a lack of distinctive style.

Finally, it must be said that like most interesting writers—surely this would be true of Hemingway and Faulkner—Brautigan's bad writing makes a more effective Brautigan parody than any conscious parody of his supposed style. *The Abortion* is such a low-keyed book that Brautigan frequently walks a tightrope between subdued drama and essentially inert or static material. A good bad example of the latter, I think, is the narrator's page-long speech to Vida (the longest single block of dialogue in the book), just before they go to bed together for the first time, in which he urges Vida "to appreciate and use" her body (67). Here, the narrator, though doubtless full of good intentions, goes on so long and so tritely that we almost suspect that Brautigan is making fun of him. But in the context of the relationship between the librarian and Vida—she more or less takes his advice, after all—such mockery can scarcely be to Brautigan's purpose.

Whether Walker Percy's parody of Brautigan is brilliant or dismal is not, of course, nearly as significant as the fact of Brautigan being accorded the left-handed honor of parody in the august pages of the Sunday *New York Times* Book Review section. This fact, as I've said, shows unmistakably that Brautigan has come to the attention of the literary Establishment (whatever *that* is).[2]

And even if Percy's parody fizzles pretty badly, as I think, there are some negative criticisms to be made of *The Abortion*. Although the novel has many pleasures, I don't think it is one of Brautigan's best books. The main problem, in my opinion, is that *The Abortion* reads almost like two different novels uneasily joined together. The opening situation—that strange library for losers, supported (off and on, more or less) by a mysterious foundation—is wonderful and very rich in possibilities. But Brautigan only develops it to a certain point and then almost seems to lose interest in it. He tantalizes us with the enigmatic American Forever foundation and with the strange apparent parallel between librarians and American presidents—but then he lets the whole thing go, shutting us out of the fable that seemed to be shaping up, as the narrator himself is finally shut out of the library by his fierce self-appointed successor.

Foster's role in *The Abortion* seems to me to be insufficiently developed also. "That Foster!" says the narrator (80), in the sort of exclamation that Walker Percy bases his parody on. The narrator tells us a lot about Foster, and we're evidently supposed to feel the great vitality and exuberance of this "caveman," to share the narrator's certainty that Foster's "heart was as big as a cantaloupe" (118). But in fact we don't really see very much of Foster. He's almost like the friend of a friend that we've heard a lot about but never met. We're *told* about him, rather than shown him in action, and as a result Foster doesn't quite come alive as a character.

In a different way, I think Brautigan's presentation of his heroine, the self-conscious sex-goddess Vida, raises a problem. In addition to the guided tour up and down her body that the narrator gives us when he describes his undressing of Vida, we see plenty of her in the book, God knows. But it seems to me that she never really becomes much more than a stereotype: the *Playboy* bunny with a sensitive soul (but, as anyone who reads the texts accompanying *Playboy's* centerfolds knows, *all* Playmates of the Month have sensitive souls). Indeed there are *four* references to *Playboy* itself scattered through the various descriptions of Vida and her spectacular effect on men. It might be said, of course, that the narrator's depiction of Vida is dramatically justified; Vida's chief complaint, after all, is that all men respond to her amazing body in the predictable terms of standard erotic fantasy. However, if the relationship between the narrator and Vida is to work—if we are to regard the narrator as in some sense heroic in his ability to respond to the *human* in people—then we have to assume that he is truly able to perceive the captive gentle spirit locked up in the castle of Vida's lush body. Perhaps he does, but Brautigan is unable to fully communicate this perception through his narrator.

Another problem in *The Abortion,* I think, is its very leisurely pace, especially in the last two-thirds of the novel. As I've said, *The Abortion* is Brautigan's longest book so far, by a good margin, and it is also the one in which the least happens. This leisurely, at times almost uneventful pace can be in large measure justified by Brautigan's anti-dramatic, anti-heroic theme. But even after saying this, it seems to me that one would have to admit that some of the episodes are merely inert, without much interest or significance. For example, the five page chapter, "The Man from Guadalajara" (159–63), deals with the arrival of the narrator and Vida in Tijuana, their chance meeting with a friendly gentleman from

Guadalajara, and his offer of a lift into downtown Tijuana, which they accept. There's almost nothing in the chapter that couldn't have been profitably abridged or omitted.

In quite a few places in *The Abortion,* Brautigan lingers to describe a scene or to transcribe a conversation that might better have been summarized. To me, this problem is the other side of Brautigan's wonderful knack for bringing the trivial or incidental alive. In his fiction and in his poetry, Brautigan seems always eager to use whatever's at hand (or in mind) as a descriptive detail or as the basis for a poem. As I said in my discussion of his poems, it sometimes appears that Brautigan believes that any group of words or sounds has intrinsic interest. In *Rommel Drives on Deep into Egypt,* for instance, he has a poem that reads:

> I feel so bad today
> that I want to write a poem.
> I don't care: any poem, this poem
> ("April 7, 1969," *Rommel Drives,* 54).

The kind of deliberate unselectivity implied in this poem —"any poem"—is perhaps responsible for some of the occasions when *The Abortion* seems to bog down.

Often for Brautigan a poem consists of whatever happens along. In his other book of poetry, *The Pill Versus the Springhill Mine Disaster,* he makes an amusing little poem ("San Francisco") out of a note he says he found scribbled on a paper bag in a laundromat. And, of course, sometimes a poem doesn't even have to have any words; thus, as I've said, in *Rommel Drives,* Brautigan includes (if that's the word) four poems for which he provides titles followed by blank pages. Perhaps the most extreme example of Brautigan's apparent belief that everything is intrinsically interesting comes from his recent LP-album, *Listening to Richard Brautigan,* on two bands of which we get to hear Brautigan doing things like taking off his clothes (rustle, rustle), brushing his teeth (scritch, scritch, scritch), and taking a bath (splash, splash)—some of "the sounds of my life," as he calls them. In *The Abortion* this fascination with everything and anything leads not only to a lack of proportion but to some rather tedious passages. Brautigan's narrator in the novel more or less expresses this problem himself, when after a brief, inconsequential description of some of the contents of the Woolworth's in Tijuana, he says, "What a bunch of junk to remember, but that's what I remember . . ." (166).

After criticizing various aspects of *The Abortion* and even after conceding that it is not one of Brautigan's very best books, I think there still remain quite a few things to praise in the novel. I wish, as I've said, that Brautigan had done more with the library situation in *The Abortion.* But as far as it goes that section of the book is really well done. Brautigan's ability to be tender without lapsing into sentimentality is evident in the opening scene between the narrator and Mrs. Charles Fine Adams, the eighty-year-old lady who has written *Growing Flowers by Candlelight in Hotel Rooms.* And that fine, warm episode is neatly balanced by the sad and zany later scene in which a madwoman shows up at the library bearing a book of blank pages, which she tears to pieces as she disappears up the street, shouting, "It isn't right that I should end up like this, doing those crazy things that I do, feeling the way that I do, saying these things" (100). In the later parts of *The Abortion,* the entire sequence at the abortionist's office is handled with understated dramatic force, particularly, as I've

87

suggested, the part when the narrator waits for the operation to be over.

But of course to go on listing effective scenes in *The Abortion* would only be to say positively what I've been saying negatively: that parts of the novel work better than the book as a whole. Similarly, despite some trivial or even tedious passages of description and dialogue, there are also many places in *The Abortion* where Brautigan uses details brilliantly. For instance, in one very brief passage he is able to convey the narrator's extreme though understated anxiety about the new experience of flying: "A small airliner about the size of a P-38 with rusty looking propellers taxied by us to take off. Its windows were filled with terrified passengers" (140). Examples of freshly observed details used with economy and wit could be culled from virtually every page of *The Abortion*, as from most of the pages of all of Brautigan's novels—the lemon peel "like flowers in the ice" of the martinis the narrator, Vida, and Foster drink to celebrate the beginning of their new, post-library lives (224); a girl's sweater looking "helpless" on the backseat of a car parked in front of the abortionist's office (168); the sprawl of daisies in front of the library, "like a Rorschach dress pattern designed by Rudi Gernreich" (34). . . . Brautigan surely belongs to that large group of American novelists referred to by the critic V. S. Pritchett when he said, ". . . always in American novels, the impedimentâ are good. Sears Roebuck has made its contribution to literature."[3]

In a very condescending, almost contemptuous review of *The Abortion*, Jonathan Yardley has written, "the harshest critical guns must be muffled in bemused sweetness by someone of such overweaning ingenuousness. . . ."[4] I don't find Brautigan such a frail blossom as is implied in a nasty phrase like "overweaning ingenuousness." I have taken quite a few critical pot shots at *The Abortion* here, for I believe the novel is very uneven and not really successful as a whole. But even if my shots have been well placed, I believe that much of the book remains intact. In its best moments—and it has quite a few good ones—*The Abortion* is a novel of both charm and complexity, which offers a moving fable of our time, which presents an unheroic but very humane hero of our time.

Chapter Four.
A Confederate General in Ruins:
A Confederate General from Big Sur

Brautigan's earliest published novel, *A Confederate General from Big Sur* (1964), resembles in several respects his most recent one, *The Abortion*. The most obvious similarity between the two books is that their respective narrators are very much alike—gentle, shy, rather anxious, even somewhat withdrawn young men "not at home in the world." In addition, in each novel the narrator is paired with a much more boisterous, extroverted partner, though in *The Abortion*, as I've said, this relationship is not fully developed. Unlike *In Water-melon Sugar*, *Confederate General* and *The Abortion* are both predominately realistic; unlike *Trout Fishing in America*, both novels follow a more or less continuous, coherent narrative. Also, as might be expected, some of the themes I've discussed in *The Abortion* are present in *Confederate General* as well. Finally, just as Brautigan seems to have shifted the focus of his attention in *The Abortion* from one kind of novel to another (from the library fable to the abortion journey), so in *Confederate General* he starts off writing a comic burlesque and winds up writing a strangely melancholy love story.

As in *The Abortion*, this fragmentation, this sense of two rather different books being joined together, takes away from the overall effectiveness of *Confederate General*. Nevertheless, the things that do work in this novel work very well indeed. Partly, I suppose, because *Confederate General* was Brautigan's first book to appear under the imprint of a publisher with national distribution, it has been pretty much ignored by the critics (even by those few who have given Brautigan respectful, sympathetic attention). But it is probably Brautigan's funniest book; at its best *Confederate General* might be described as a comic burlesque of "America After the War Between the States."

The main plot action of *Confederate General* is simple and can be quickly summarized. As always in Brautigan (one of several things he has in common with Mark Twain), how the tale is told is at least as important as what happens in it. The narrator, Jesse, meets another young man, named Lee Mellon, in San Francisco. Lee has just extorted some money from a wealthy homosexual who had wanted him "to commit an act of oral outrage" (21), but settled, rather cheerfully, for a bash on the head instead. Lee moves into the strange boarding house that Jesse lives in, where he has a very brief (three-day) affair with a sixteen-year-old girl who, as we later learn, becomes pregnant. When his money is all gone, Lee moves to Oakland, where he lives rent-free in the house of a friend who's in a mental hospital. For light and heat, Lee taps a gas line of the Pacific Gas & Electric Company; he scrounges his food.

After a while, restless Lee Mellon moves on again, this time to Big Sur, where he lives in a cabin owned by yet another unbalanced friend. Later Jesse joins Lee at Big Sur, after a lengthy exchange of letters between the two men; among other things, we learn from these letters that Jesse is suffering from the effects of an unhappy love affair. Life in their Pacific paradise is somewhat complicated by an absence of money, and by the presence, in a nearby pond, of 7,452 frogs, whose nightly croaking threatens to drive Jesse and Lee crazy.

But then their luck changes. They come into some money ($6.72), which they take from two teenage boys whom they catch trying to steal gasoline from Lee's truck. With this windfall they rush off to Monterey—where Lee immediately gets drunk and passes out, but where Jesse meets a pleasant, attractive young girl named Elaine. Elaine returns to Big Sur with Jesse and Lee the next day, bringing bags and bags of groceries and two alligators. The alligators take care of the frog problem, Elaine moves into Jesse's cabin with him, and when Elizabeth—a radiantly beautiful free spirit who works three months a year as a high-priced prostitute—arrives to comfort Lee, everything seems completely idyllic.

However, at this point (about two-thirds of the way through *Confederate General*), like a fifth wheel on Lee Mellon's old homemade truck, Johnston Wade, a crazed, middle-aged insurance executive shows up, seeking sanctuary from his wife and children, who want to put him in a mental hospital. Wade arrives bearing two bottles of bourbon, $100,000 in cash, and a ten-cent pomegranate; he makes his appearance in a brand-new expensive sports car (his "Bentley Bomb"), which he's attempting to conceal under felled trees when Jesse and Lee come upon him.

After disrupting the serenity of life at Big Sur for a couple of days, Wade suddenly snaps back into sanity, as it seems, and hurries off to keep an important business appointment. The two young couples go down to the edge of the Pacific to "turn on and go with the waves" (151). Jesse and Elaine go off to make love, but Jesse can't get an erection. *Confederate General* ends . . . well, it doesn't exactly *end;* instead the novel whirls away to various alternate endings and then finally to what Brautigan calls "186,000 endings per second" (159). I'll have more to say later about these endings.

Like much of Brautigan's work, *Confederate General* belongs, at least partly, to a broad category of American literature—stories dealing with a man going off alone (or two men going off together), away from the complex problems and frustrations of society into a simpler world close to nature, whether in the woods, in the mountains, on the river, wherever. We might call this pattern American Pastoral. As Leslie Fiedler notes in his fine book, *Love and Death in the American Novel,* this theme of man/men fleeing society is at the heart of many American literary classics. In fact, Fiedler finds the legend of "Rip Van Winkle"—the man who cops out of his domestic duties by boozing off to sleep in the mountains—to be the central myth of our literature.[1]

The difference between Rip Van Winkle asleep in the mountains and Henry Thoreau wide awake at Walden Pond is, after all, only one of degree, or life-style. Both men have withdrawn from, or dropped out of, their immediate societies.

More characteristically in American literature, however, the escape from society is a two-man job. From the numerous examples that come to mind—Huck and Jim on the river in *Huckleberry Finn,* Jake and Bill fishing in the mountains of Spain in Hemingway's *The Sun Also Rises*—perhaps the best models for the two-man American Pastoral are Natty Bumpo and Chingachgook, in James Fennimore Cooper's Leather-Stocking Novels. Natty (like his real-life prototype, Daniel Boone) is driven by the need to move further westward each time he hears the sound of an ax announcing the advance of civilization. This impulse has its comic parallel in *Confederate General,* for Jesse and Lee first become aware of Johnston Wade's disruptive presence when they are awakened by "a chopping sound," Wade cutting down trees to conceal his car. The main reason that Brautigan's novel fits only partly into the American Pastoral category is that usually such works are sexless, no women allowed, while in *Confederate General* Elaine and Elizabeth are present for much of the book, and, at first anyway, their presence seems anything but disruptive.

Brautigan is not, of course, the first American writer to locate his Paradise Regained in Big Sur. Within the last fifteen years, two other books about Big Sur and bearing an important relationship to *Confederate General* have appeared: Henry Miller's *Big Sur and the Oranges of Hieronymus Bosch* (1957) and Jack Kerouac's *Big Sur* (1962). Kerouac's painful novel is a virtually undisguised account of the author's attempts to find peace and serenity in an isolated cabin above the beach at Big Sur. Arriving exhausted in body and soul by the harassments that have followed closely upon his literary fame, Dulouz, Kerouac's autobiographical narrator, does find peace, for a very brief time. But by his fourth day at Big Sur he is amazed to find himself already bored. For the rest of the novel, Dulouz bounces back and forth between Big Sur and San Francisco (and other California towns), becoming increasingly desperate and depressed. After a long dark night of sleeplessness and paranoia, Dulouz recovers enough equilibrium to return east, which of course is where he began his quest for peace in the first place. The road finally leads nowhere. As Dulouz says, "The circle's closed in on the old heroes of the night."[2] In contrast to Brautigan's zany but pleasant Big Sur, Kerouac's is alternately a place of boredom and terror.

It's appropriate, if coincidental, that in both *Confederate General* and *Big Sur* the authors make explicit reference to Henry Miller. At one point in *Big Sur*, Dulouz mentions self-importantly that he was supposed to drop in on Henry Miller. Instead, though, he decides to telephone him at around ten p.m., only to learn that poor old Henry is already preparing for bed. In *Confederate General*, on the other hand, Jesse points out Miller's old Cadillac to Elaine, as they drive past it on the way back to Big Sur from Monterey. There's no question of dropping in on or even of calling up "poor old Henry." Jesse, in fact, mentions Miller very casually, as he'd point out a deer or any interesting sight along the road. And Elaine reacts just right by not reacting at all. "Oh," she says (95). The point here is that Brautigan's characters belong in their Big Sur paradise. They're not interested in status or in Henry Miller's literary reputation, or in any of that. Dulouz mentions Miller as if to show his own importance, thus further showing that he has not shaken free of the very things he thinks he's running away from: status, prestige. Dulouz, like Emerson's American tourist in Europe, has brought his own ruins to Big Sur with him.

The gigantic figure of Henry Miller casts its long shadow across *Confederate General*, as it has across so many American books in the last twenty or twenty-five years. In some respects, Brautigan's Big Sur corresponds closely to Miller's—a place of beauty and privacy and freedom and (that word and quality Miller likes so much) ambience. For the most part, Jesse and Lee act out the advice that Miller repeats to himself and to us in the first section of his *Big Sur: "Stay put and watch the world go round!"*[3] Advice, it need hardly be said, as much directed to the head and soul as to the legs and body.

Even if we suspect that Henry Miller has served at least partly as Brautigan's literary guide to Big Sur, however, Brautigan's depiction of Jesse and Lee's Eden is ultimately very different from Miller's (or anyone's). For in *Confederate General* everything comes through the unique perceptions of the narrator, Jesse. At one point in the novel, Jesse, commenting on the impossibly bad bread baked by Lee Mellon, says, "What a wonderful sense of distortion Lee Mellon had" (82). Actually, though, this remark is at least as true of Jesse as of Lee. Throughout *Confederate General*, we get experience, reality, filtered through Jesse's "sense of distortion," which is to say, through his imagination.

The whole framework of Brautigan's novel—the Confederate General motif—is a product of Jesse's sense of distortion. Lee Mellon believes that his great grandfather, Augustus Mellon, was a gallant Confederate general. He holds to this belief tenaciously, even after he and Jesse are unable to find any reference to a General Mellon, C.S.A., in the book *Generals in Gray*, which they examine at the San Francisco public library. Lee himself is clearly something of a secessionist, rebel, outlaw, or maybe just a drop-out. Jesse puts the two things together —the supposed military career of Augustus Mellon and the actual exploits of Lee Mellon—and, with typical Brautigan logic (which often, as here, fuses things that have only a very improbable or tenuous connection), he leaps to the imaginative vision of Big Sur as the twelfth member of the Confederate States of America; then, extending the fantasy, Jesse further imagines the area patriotically sending a contingent of troops to assist Robert E. Lee's Army of Northern Virginia: the 8th Big Sur Volunteer Heavy Root Eaters, primitive and placid Digger Indians, equipped with roots and limpets.

More important than his role as catalyst of this zany fantasy is the way Lee Mellon is used by Brautigan to burlesque various entrenched American myths. Most obviously, Lee is a comic version of the man of action, the Confederate General from Big Sur, a hundred years too late, whose military forays consist in things like beating the Pacific Gas & Electric Company by tapping a gas main. Jesse refers to his account of Lee Mellon as "this military narrative" (19), and throughout Lee's adventures are described as "skirmishes." Lee struggles, however, not against the G.A.R., but against the P.G.E. His adventures are distinctly mock-heroic.

Similarly, Lee Mellon bears a comic resemblance to the romantic outlaw figure. When Lee and Jesse are terrorizing the two teenage boys they catch trying to steal their gasoline—Lee armed with an empty rifle,

Jesse with an axe—Jesse says, "Do you see how perfect our names were, how the names lent themselves to this kind of business?" (78). Jesse and Lee—like a pair of legendary desperadoes straight out of Robert Coates' *The Outlaw Years*. Only, Lee's deeds as an outlaw don't go beyond extorting a few dollars from the boys in the gasoline episode or shaking down a wealthy homosexual. Once again we are dealing with mock-heroic, with burlesque.

Lee's most significant role in Brautigan's comic deflation of American myths (a role that overlaps his rebel and outlaw manifestations) is Lee Mellon as the self-reliant, jack-of-all-trades, democratic hero, the conqueror of the wilderness. Lee belongs to that line of independent, resourceful Americans which the narrator of Ralph Ellison's *Invisible Man* calls the tradition of "thinker-tinkers," highly practical men who are also visionaries. But, once again, Lee represents a burlesque of the type. Ellison's Invisible Man provides himself with 1,369 electric lights at the expense of Monopolated Light & Power; Lee Mellon, as I've said, tunnels into a gas line of Pacific Gas & Electricity. But, where Ellison's narrator makes efficient use of the power he taps, exploiting the exploiter, Lee never quite gets "the energy to put the thing under complete control" (44); as a result, he loses his eyebrows to the six-foot blue flame that shoots out every time he turns the gas on. Lee provides shelter by building his own cabin at Big Sur, but (due to gin and impatience) it turns out to have a ceiling only five-feet one-inch high, leading to incessant knocks on the head. He provides food, which Jesse describes as "a perfect gastronomical Hiroshima" (68). For transportation, Lee builds his own truck, which looks "just like a Civil War truck, if they'd had trucks back in those

98

times" (82–3); he also has a motorcycle, in numerous pieces scattered around Jesse's cabin. When Lee Mellon requires tobacco, he walks the highway overlooking the Pacific ("Like a kind of weird Balboa . . . ."), searching for butts; Jesse imagines Lee walking in vain all the way north to Seattle, then east all the way to New York, and not finding a single cigarette butt: "Not a damn one, and the end of an American dream" (105). And the end of an American Dream is exactly the point. When Jesse comes to retrieve Lee from under the cardboard he'd used to conceal him after Lee passed out, Jesse describes him as "the end product of American spirit, pride and the old know-how" (93).

Lee Mellon is not the only character Brautigan uses to burlesque American myths. Johnston Wade is important here too. As I've said, Wade arrives at Big Sur as an ominous echo of civilization: "hackEty/wackEty: CHOP!"(117). When Lee and Jesse first come upon him he is feverishly chopping down trees to hide the expensive new car in which he has fled the machinations of his wife and children, who want to have him committed. And Wade *is* crazy, or at least most of the time he is. Like many other products of the American Dream, he seems to have been driven to madness by the contrast between the illusion of success and its realities.

Wade is the president of the Johnston Wade Insurance Company—a big shot, a success, a self-made man. A self-made man on the run—Babbitt as Rip Van Winkle, Leslie Fiedler might say—seeking refuge in an Eden of social drop-outs. Lee and Jesse immediately and simultaneously rename Wade "Roy Earle," the Bogart outlaw-hero of the movie *High Sierra,* who is hunted down and killed in the California mountains. As Jesse explains—another good example of Brautigan logic—"The man sort

99

of looked like Humphrey Bogart in *High Sierra*, except that he was short, fat, bald-headed and looked like a guilty businessman . . ." (119).

The transformation of Johnston Wade into Roy Earle is more than mere whimsy. For, as much as Lee Mellon, Wade is an embodiment of "the end of an American dream." Whereas Lee is a comic portrayal of the self-reliant man *outside* of society—adventurer, swaggerer, outlaw, rebel—Wade is a sad comic representative of the self-made man who has made it *within* society: a successful businessman with an expensive home and a family—a family, however, that "want to lock Pop up . . ." (123). Appropriately, the chapter in which we get most of Wade's background is called "A Short History of America After the War Between the States." Paralleling the image of Lee Mellon forever wandering the highways of America in search of cigarette butts is that of Johnston Wade careening madly through the American night in his "Bentley Bomb," clutching his briefcase containing $100,000 and a ten-cent pomegranate.

The very first words of *Confederate General*—the chapter-heading "Attrition's Old Sweet Song"—are pertinent to Johnston Wade's role in the novel. Brautigan begins the book with a tabulation of the 126 Confederate generals who were not in rank at the end of the Civil War, for causes ranging from "Killed in Action or Died of Wounds" (seventy-seven) down to "Committed Suicide," "Dropped," "Reverted to Rank of Colonel" (one each). Wade is a kind of captain (if not quite general) of the business world whose "attrition" has been caused by the pressures and disillusionments of American life "After the War Between the States." Among the alternate endings Brautigan provides for *Confederate General*, one has Wade searching frantically for his ten-cent pomegranate ("It's going to Los Angeles with me. Big Business" [157]), which would seem to indicate a resumption of his "sane" life as an acquisitive businessman. But another ending depicts Wade, Lee, and Elizabeth flinging hundred-dollar bills—Wade's $100,000 hoard—into the Pacific ("All this money ever did was bring me here" (158)), which implies an "insane" repudiation of his business life. Since these are only two possible alternate endings (out of an equally possible 186,000 endings per second), we're left with the idea that the Civil War within Johnston Wade/Roy Earle will rage on.

Important as Johnston Wade is as a thematic foil, the civil war within him is, of course, a relatively minor skirmish in *Confederate General*. We are much more concerned with Wade's "amigo," Lee Mellon—that "Lee-of-another-color"—and his role in the book. As I've said, Jesse maintains an intermittent parallel between the comic exploits of Lee Mellon and the imaginary adventures of Lee's illustrious ancestor, Augustus Mellon—the non-Confederate-general, who was not from Big Sur (but who was supposed to have had a statue erected to him somewhere in the South, which nobody could ever find). About two-thirds of the way through *Confederate General*, Jesse begins conjuring up regular episodes from *Private* Augustus Mellon's participation in the Battle of the Wilderness. These vignettes are terse and mostly pretty grim; some of them are curiously reminiscent of the inter-chapters in Hemingway's *In Our Time*. Taken together these episodes, dealing with one of the bloodiest battles of the Civil War, might even remind the reader of the section in Stephen Crane's *Red Badge of Courage* in which young Henry Fleming wanders alone through a forest after becoming separated from his regiment, constantly in close proximity to death. In fact Brautigan

101

shows a versatility he's not generally given credit for in catching some of the flavor of actual chronicles of the Battle of the Wilderness.[4] Yet the last of these vignettes takes us all the way back to the beginning of *Confederate General,* back to Jesse's cheerful fantasy of the peaceful Heavy Root Eaters arriving from Big Sur to comfort General Lee and his horse. Augustus Mellon, wearing a pair of boots he took from a decapitated Union officer, stumbles into a clearing where *"the 8th Big Sur Volunteer Heavy Root Eaters began dancing in a circle, the general and his horse in the middle, while all around them waged the American Civil War, the last good time this country ever had"* (147).

Within the charmed circle of the Digger Indians—so indolent, says Jesse, that they don't even "give birth to their children" (16)—Augustus Mellon is a survivor. The increasingly grim details of the bloody battle dissolve into fantasy and farce. Similarly, Lee Mellon—who finally resembles the Diggers rather more than he resembles his namesake, General Robert E. Lee—is a survivor. His triumph in the twentieth-century Wilderness, "After the War Between the States," is essentially one of passive resistance; he endures. It is appropriate that the very first thing Jesse tells us about Lee Mellon is that he "has a truly gifted faculty for getting his teeth knocked out" (19). And so he does, having gone through 175 of them in five years, by Jesse's count. Yet Lee always has a few teeth in his mouth, or, at very least, a toothless plate, "just so he would have a head start on the gristle" (20). Lee may be mostly toothless, but he goes on chewing.

Lee Mellon's persistence or tenacity is directly related to one of the recurrent statements in *Confederate General:* "man is the dominant creature on this shit pile."

Lee himself first says this, after the alligators have freed Jesse and Lee from the tyranny of frogs (97). Later, Jesse repeats Lee's assertion to himself to keep his courage up as he goes nervously into the darkness to investigate the mysterious chopping noises. Finally, at the very end of the book, pestered by flies as he tries unsuccessfully to make love to Elaine, Jesse puts the statement interrogatively and bitterly: "Who said we were the dominant creature on this shit pile?" (156).

As in *The Abortion*—indeed, as in much of his work —Brautigan is concerned in *Confederate General* with the theme of *dominance*, in the sense of controlling or coping with one's life. And in *Confederate General*, even more than in *The Abortion* perhaps, this question of control is a very chancy business. Against Lee Mellon's dubious assertion about man's dominance, we can balance a recurrent detail from the very beginning of Jesse's adventures at Big Sur. After banging his head (not for the first time) on Lee's absurdly low ceiling, Jesse watches some insects on a log he's put on the fire. Four times, within three pages, he thinks, *"The bugs were standing there on the log looking out at us through the fire"* (60-62). The utter helplessness of insects caught on a burning log . . . a natural metaphor for the inability of people to control their lives. Indeed, this is exactly the way Hemingway uses the recollection of Frederick Henry (in *A Farewell to Arms*) of having dropped a log full of ants on a fire once, a recollection that comes to him as he waits helplessly for his lover, Catherine, to die. In *Confederate General* it might be said that the human condition is somewhere between dominant creature and helpless bug.

Although Lee's "campaign" victories (such as the one over the Pacific Gas & Electric Co., in which he loses

103

his eyebrows) are as incomplete as his dental structure, Jesse is not nearly as successful as Lee at coping with life. Jesse's strange melancholy, which colors virtually the entire book and comes to dominate it more and more, is one of the most perplexing and, I think, one of the least satisfactory aspects of *Confederate General*.

Like the narrators of many other American novels (for instance, Hawthorne's *Blithedale Romance*, whose reticent narrator, Coverdale, he resembles in some respects), Jesse is a character who tells us more about what he sees than about who he is. We learn about Jesse only gradually and in bits and pieces, and perhaps even at the end of *Confederate General* we remain puzzled by him. In the early parts of the novel he functions mainly as Lee Mellon's chronicler and straight man; he's almost like the perennial sidekick in old-fashioned Westerns who gets to hold the hero's horse (or guitar) in the kissing scenes.

As I've said, Jesse has a lot of things in common with the librarian-narrator in *The Abortion*. Both men are lonely and shy, losers who identify with losers. In the first part of *Confederate General*, Jesse lives in a boarding house, appropriately located on Leavenworth Street, which suggests his imprisonment in loneliness. At the boarding house, Jesse's best friend (or, to put it more accurately, the closest thing he has to a friend) is an eighty-four-year-old spinster, who lives (Jesse believes/ imagines) on a pension of thirty-five cents a month, a woman so old and so alone that she has come to seem nonhuman, has come to resemble The Heap, a comic-book hero of Jesse's childhood. For Jesse, this old woman stands for all the lonely old people across the United States. His reference to the hotplate on which she does her "cooking" (quotation marks are needed here because she lives chiefly on celery root) is a good example of the way Brautigan can use detail: "A hotplate in a little room is the secret flower of millions of old people in this country" (37). Jesse, of course, is drawn to the old woman's loneliness, just as the narrator of *The Abortion* is drawn to the lonely souls who bring their unwanted books to his library.

In the same section of *Confederate General*, Jesse makes it clear that his feelings toward lonely losers come from a sense of identification rather than from pity. He tells us that he sometimes goes to see triple-features at run-down movie theaters, "to confuse my senses" (42). At these places he joins the company of "the sailors who can't get laid, the old people who make those theaters their solariums, the immobile visionaries, and the poor sick people who come there for the outpatient treatment of watching a pair of Lusitanian mammary glands kiss a set of Titanic capped teeth" (42–3).

Jesse himself might be called a kind of "immobile visionary." Certainly he has very little of the audacity of spirit he admires in Lee Mellon. The main humor in "The Letters of Arrival and Reply" between Jesse and Lee, before Jesse goes to join Lee at Big Sur, comes from the contrast between their priorities. Jesse, unlucky in love and "looking for a way out" (52), is nevertheless anxious about such basic things as shelter, warmth, food —with practical matters: "How do we keep alive at Big Sur?" (59). On the other hand, although he constantly exhorts Jesse to "bring whiskey," Lee proudly depicts his ramshackle hideaway as a transcendentalist's paradise, as a place where one's soul has room "to get outside its marrow" (54). Lee writes, "I've got a garden that grows all year round! a 30:30 Winchester for deer, a .22 for rabbits and quail. I've got some fishing tackle and *The Journal of Albion Moonlight*" (59). And his catalogue seems to imply the rhetorical question, Who could ask for anything more?

After Jesse joins Lee at Big Sur, the contrast between their personalities becomes even more dramatic. Like the narrator in *The Abortion*, Jesse has a very active "granny gland." He implores Lee not to shoot up their last five bullets "in one thrill-crazed flurry" (65), but reckless Lee nevertheless goes off hunting, "taking with him all the bullets we had in the world" (65). When they finally get their hands on some money (the $6.72 from the teenage boys), Jesse is determined to use it for such things as rice, hamburger, and bullets; Lee counters, "Let's take this money and get laid . . . . I think that's more important than food or bullets" (82).

Anxious Practical-Pig though he may be, Jesse—still in the classic Western movie-mold—is completely loyal to Lee Mellon. Upon their first meeting, he tells us directly, ". . . I wanted to be his friend" (24). While they are both living in the boarding house on Leavenworth Street, Lee gets a young girl named Susan pregnant, and when she comes around looking for Lee, Jesse lies about his friend's whereabouts, even after Susan has "found out the score," and the lie has become a joke between them. On the night Jesse meets Elaine, he reluctantly leaves her friendly bed to retrieve Lee from under the cardboard he'd covered him with when Lee passed out. Throughout *Confederate General* Jesse follows Lee's leads, however hare-brained, backs him up, sticks up for him.

So far, it would appear as if Jesse were merely Lee Mellon's devoted sidekick, the Sancho Panza to Lee's American Quixote. And perhaps *Confederate General* would be a more completely successful novel if this were the case. But, as the book develops, Jesse himself becomes more and more the focal character. The story becomes his story rather than a story told by him. As I've said, Jesse is strangely melancholy, and his melancholy very much colors the final effect of *Confederate General*.

Jesse's envy of the relationship between Lee and Susan is played down (though, in fact, it is his discovery of them in bed together that sends him off to the movies to confuse his senses). Later, Jesse's unhappy affair with Cynthia ("just plain hell with onions on it" (52)) is entirely offstage, so to speak, since we learn about it only through a series of predominantly comic letters; we never see Jesse and Cynthia together. But from about the middle of *Confederate General*—when Jesse meets Elaine—Jesse's role as the aspiring romantic who's generally unsuccessful in life and love and can't believe his luck when things do go well becomes an important factor in the novel.

In the paragraph just before he describes how he came to meet Elaine, Jesse says, "I was pretending very hard that I was a human being . . ." (88). At about this point, if not earlier, we begin to see Jesse as a person maintaining a very precarious balance. Perhaps we might even go back a couple of chapters, to the odd and funny episode in which Jesse describes his nightly ritual at Big Sur: counting the punctuation marks in Ecclesiastes. Jesse explains his absorption with periods, commas, and so forth, as "just putting in time" (71). But his concentration on Ecclesiastes seems to be a method of maintaining his stability by performing a mechanical task. Ecclesiastes, of course, provided the title for Hemingway's *The Sun Also Rises*, and Brautigan's "The Rivets in Ecclesiastes" reminds me once again of Hemingway—this time of his famous "Big Two-Hearted River." In that story, Nick, a young man shattered in mind and spirit, tries to regain his grip by the careful, precise execution of basic tasks—setting up a camp, preparing a meal, rigging fishing equipment. Jesse's task is meaningless, ridiculous even, but it seems to have the same therapeutic effect that Nick's chores have on him. To me, the last sentence of the "Ecclesiastes" chapter in *Confederate General* reads very much like a conscious parody of "Big Two-Hearted River": "I counted the punctuation marks in Ecclesiastes very carefully so as not to make a mistake, and then I blew the lantern out" (75).

As pleasant as Jesse's relationship with Elaine is for him, and as pleased as it makes him "to be pleased again" (92), we are prepared, surely, for him to be very anxious about the affair. At the very beginning of the relationship Jesse refers to himself self-deprecatingly as "the Horatio Alger of Casanovas" (92). As I've said he can hardly believe his luck: "Jesse's got a girl . . ." (89). The very first morning at Big Sur, Jesse wakes up to find that Elaine is not in the sleeping bag with him, and he's "startled" (107). He assumes, automatically, that she's gone.

When Elizabeth shows up, things become further complicated for Jesse. Elizabeth is beautiful and serene; she has the same dazzling appeal as Vida in *The Abortion*, without Vida's insecurity and bitterness. She both attracts and daunts Jesse. "Her beauty," he says, "made me feel disconsolate" (110). Although Jesse doesn't try to make love to Elizabeth—he's held back by shyness and by loyalty (to Lee as well as to Elaine)—he does become virtually obsessed with her. "I wondered what Elizabeth was doing," Jesse says at the very end of

Confederate General (155), even as Elaine tries to arouse him sexually. Earlier, he jumps to the wildly irrational conclusion that Elizabeth is sharing a sleeping bag with (of all people!) Johnston Wade. "Why should I think that?" he wonders (144).

As Jesse yearns for the inaccessible Elizabeth and worries about losing the accessible Elaine, things begin to slip away from him. He comes to feel "a sudden wave of vacancy go over me, like a hotel being abandoned by its guests for an obvious reason" (149). A few pages later, Jesse adds, "I was really gone" (152). In the final chapter, Jesse is unable to get an erection, even with the affectionate assistance of Elaine. As the novel ends, Jesse seems to be slipping further and further away.

The ending/endings of *Confederate General* might appear to be a mere gimmick or a put-on: five alternate endings, all beginning with Jesse's depression and Elaine's attempt to cheer him up, followed by a whirl-away to "more endings, faster and faster until this book is having 186,000 endings per second" (159). But I think that insofar as the novel does become essentially Jesse's story the speed-of-light proliferation of endings is appropriate and meaningful. Just as the alternate endings (searching for his pomegranate, flinging away his money) indicate the conflict within Johnston Wade, so too they suggest Jesse's uncertainty and his inability to cope with his life. The final proliferation, that is to say, parallels the sense of confusion within Jesse. It's significant that Lee, Elizabeth, and Elaine (the more or less stable characters) are essentially unaffected by the different endings, while Jesse and Johnston Wade assume differing roles in the various endings. In all of them, however,

Jesse presents himself as passive, oddly detached, almost dazed.

We might remember here that one of Lee Mellon's few possessions is a copy of Kenneth Patchen's *The Journal of Albion Moonlight*. It seems likely that Brautigan also owns or has owned a copy of this wonderful novel, for Patchen's book has an ending that is quite similar to the wide-open ending of *Confederate General*. After his long account of real and imaginary, inner and outer joys and terrors, Albion Moonlight closes his journal by writing, ". . . *What am I going to do?*

> There is no way to end this book
> No way to begin"[5]

Mysteriously overcome, Jesse too seems to be left at the end of *Confederate General* with no way to end, no way to begin; nowhere to go, nothing to do.

But we must ask, I think, *Why* is Jesse so down? What happens to the comical sidekick? Has Sancho Panza somehow turned into Hamlet? (It's interesting that Jesse thinks of *Hamlet* as Elaine does a slow striptease before him on the beach, right near the end of the novel.) Are we supposed to assume that Jesse's relatively unaccustomed indulgence in bourbon and marijuana has had physically and psychically depressing effects on him? Is Brautigan perhaps unconsciously echoing Henry Miller's question about why certain creative and sensitive types seem ill-adapted to life at Big Sur: "Is something lacking? Or is there too much . . . too much sunshine, too much fog, too much peace and contentment?"[6]

I don't think Brautigan answers these questions; that's why I think Jesse isn't a completely successful character. It seems to me that Brautigan started with Jesse mainly as a narrator, the chronicler of Lee Mellon's comical exploits, but then became more and more interested in Jesse as a character in his own right. At any rate, Jesse's tentative explanation of his plight at the end of *Confederate General*—his physical impotence, his mental vacancy—surely seems inadequate: "A little bit too much of life had been thrown at me, and I couldn't put it all together . . . . It had been such a long hard week. I felt things slipping in my mind" (154).

In my view, then, Brautigan's novel itself, like that "toothless raider" Lee Mellon, has to be considered "a Confederate general in ruins" (18). If we agree with Jesse's description of Lee as "the battle flags and drums of this book" (18), we can only wish that Brautigan had continued to use Jesse in a supportive capacity, that he had not allowed Jesse as character to supersede Jesse as narrator.

As I have tried to show, Jesse's "campaign biography" of Lee Mellon has deep roots in American myth and rich affinities with American literary tradition. My purpose in mentioning numerous American authors who have either influenced or paralleled Brautigan's concerns in *Confederate General*—Irving, Cooper, Hemingway, Kerouac, Miller, Ellison, Patchen—was not to indulge in academic pedantry. (I haven't even mentioned Walt Whitman, and Brautigan refers to or quotes from him several times in the novel!) I think it is important to realize that Brautigan's burlesque of American destinies (and thus America's destiny) is very much in what still another author referred to in *Confederate General*, William Carlos Williams, has called "the American Grain."

In his presentation of Lee Mellon as the secessionist trying to sustain himself by his skills and wits outside of American society, Brautigan is testing one of the major themes of our literature, a theme explicitly formulated by Henry Miller, in his *Big Sur*: "For the man who wants to lead the good life, which is a way of saying *his own life*, there is always a spot where he can dig and take root."[7] In his complementary images of Lee Mellon wandering the highway and Johnston Wade careening through the night, Brautigan is asking the same question that so many American writers past and present have asked of American society; as Allen Ginsberg poses it, the question runs, "Where O America are you/ going . . .?"[8]

Despite the predominantly comic tone of *Confederate General*, in treating the possibilities of American life "After the War Between the States" mock-heroically (i.e., Lee Mellon *is* a [mostly] "toothless raider," his self-reliance is largely ludicrous), Brautigan may be said to be pessimistic or at least nostalgic. There are perhaps even moments in *Confederate General* when we might wonder whether he's being entirely ironic in calling the Civil War *"the last good time this country ever had"* (149).

In technique as well as in theme, *Confederate General* is very much in "the American Grain." As a narrator, Jesse has more than a distant relationship to the Tall Tale and Yarnspinning traditions that go far back in American literature. Exaggeration, used throughout *Confederate General* (from the old lady who lives only on celery root to Lee Mellon having lost 175 teeth), is of course the very basis of the Tall Tale. The mock-heroic aspects of *Confederate General* relate the book to such frontier classics as Johnston Jones Hooper's *Adventures of Simon Suggs* and Thomas Bangs Thorpe's "Big Bear of Arkansas." Like the finest of the native yarnspinners—men like Thorpe, George Washington Harris, most of

112

all Mark Twain—Brautigan displays a rich fertility of detail and incident throughout *Confederate General.* Moreover, Jesse's omnivorous curiosity, heightened imagination, and sense of distortion cause him frequently to digress, again like a classic yarnspinner. Occasionally, Jesse even sounds almost like Jim Blaine, the extraordinarily garrulous narrator of Mark Twain's "The Story of the Old Ram," who never quite does get around to relating "a wonderful adventure which he once had with his grandfather's old ram. . . ."[9] Brautigan does not use the technique of wandering steadily further and further away from the supposed point, as in Jim Blaine's tale, but in *Confederate General* some of the funniest passages are asides in which Jesse strays briefly from his main narrative. One of my favorite examples of this is Jesse's description of the boarding house on Leavenworth Street. After telling us that the house was owned by a Chinese dentist, he goes on to say that the dentist always wore a pair of blue overalls to collect the rent; these overalls he kept in what he called his "tool room," "but there weren't any tools there, only the blue overalls hanging on a hook" (32). Then Jesse moves on to a description of the irascible retired music teacher who'd lived below him in the boarding house. In discussing this man's sudden death, Jesse circles back to the Chinese dentist again: "I heard that it was his heart, but the way the Chinese dentist described the business, it could have been his teeth" (34).

As in *The Abortion* (only much more so), there are examples of Brautigan's good eye for details and of his sense of the incongruous on virtually every page of *Confederate General.* (The fact that there are fewer examples toward the end of the novel is in itself a good reason to lament Brautigan's shift in focus.) Flipping through the book more or less at random, I find: the disapproving librarian whose eyes "seemed to have grown a pair of eyeglasses" (30), Lee Mellon discovering (long before the botulism scare) that "Campbell's Soup!" was a phrase that frightened frogs (71), Lee Mellon's half-starved cats purring "up from the depths of their prehistoric memories a rusty old plantlike purr —they were so little used to contentment . . ." (100–1), the two pet-shop alligators emerging from their boxes and wondering what had happened to the puppies they'd been caged next to (102–3) . . . . The combination of details, imaginative vitality, and what I've previously called Brautigan logic (essentially the juxtaposition or fusion of wildly unrelated things: a fat middle-aged businessman and Humphrey Bogart) makes *Confederate General* not only Brautigan's funniest book but one of the funniest in recent American literature.

And, apart from everything else, to write a funny book is something. Once, when I was teaching *Confederate General*, I asked a student some thematic question, and he replied, "When I read this book I don't know what's going on, but I laugh my balls off."

Chapter Five.
A Delicate Balance: *In Watermelon Sugar*

Whereas Brautigan's other novels are all deeply rooted in contemporary American experience, filled with circumstantial details that give all three books vitality, *In Watermelon Sugar* (1968) is set in a strange fantasy world. In moving from Northern California to the small community of iDEATH, Brautigan relinquishes one of the chief assets of his other novels, a strong sense of time and place. The action of *In Watermelon Sugar*, in fact, seems almost to be outside of time and place. Or, rather, time and place in this novel have the shifting indefiniteness of a dream. Instead of reminding us of such cartographers of the American scene as Hemingway or Henry Miller, Brautigan's narrative technique in *In Watermelon Sugar* appears to be about halfway between Lewis Carroll and Robert Heinlein, halfway between "nonsense" fantasy and science fiction.

Despite important differences in setting, technique, and tone, however, *In Watermelon Sugar* does have affinities with Brautigan's other books. Most obviously, once again, the narrator of *In Watermelon Sugar* closely resembles the librarian in *The Abortion* and Jesse in *Confederate General*. Indeed, at about this point, we might as well start referring to the narrators of all three novels as "the Brautigan narrator"—a shy, retiring, lonely, gentle spirit, observant but not at home in the world. Based on the little that Brautigan has chosen to tell about himself, and without straining our inferences too much, we can say (for what it's worth) that this narrator is an autobiographical projection of the author, reflecting more or less directly, Brautigan's point of view, perceptions, values; revealing what Bob Dylan, in a very different context, calls a concern with "chaos, watermelons, clocks, everything."[1]

In addition to the persistence of the Brautigan narrator, one major theme of *Confederate General* is explored somewhat similarly in *In Watermelon Sugar*. The serene, gentle, uncomplicated lives of the characters in the latter novel may be seen as the fantasy equivalent of the life-style Jesse and Lee aspire to in *Confederate General;* the burlesque pastoral at Big Sur finds its serious counterpart in the idyllic iDEATH. The whimsically idealized version of the way the Digger Indians lived in *Confederate General* bears a close correspondence to the "gentle life" the narrator and his friends lead in *In Watermelon Sugar*: "they lived on roots and limpets and sat pleasantly out in the rain" (*Confederate General*, p. 16).

Although *In Watermelon Sugar* is the furthest removed from conventional realism of all Brautigan's novels, like both *The Abortion* and *Confederate General* it does have a continuous narrative line. The story, however, is structurally more complex than in the other two books, involving, for one thing, a fairly sophisticated use of flashback technique. Also, and despite the fantasy terms of the novel, the narrative (as well as the tone) is better unified in *In Watermelon Sugar* than in any of Brautigan's other books.

In Watermelon Sugar is much shorter than either *The Abortion* or *Confederate General*, but it is nevertheless a very difficult book to summarize intelligibly. Briefly, the story deals with a young man who lives in a small community (or large commune) in a sort of traumatized world, after the apparent break-up of a much larger and much more complex civilization. As in *The Abortion*, the narrator of *In Watermelon Sugar* is unnamed, but his lack of a specific name does not imply (as it did for the librarian in *The Abortion*) the absence of any identity so much as a shifting identity or a restlessness. He tells us, ". . . I am one of those who do not have a regular name. My name depends on you. Just call me whatever is in your mind"(4).

Not only the narrator's name, but many of the things in the world of *In Watermelon Sugar* constantly shift and change. The sun shines a different color each day of the week—red, golden, gray, black, white, blue and brown, Monday through Sunday—and this variation causes the watermelons, the staple crop, to grow in

117

correspondingly different colors. Similarly, the central meeting place of the characters, iDEATH, goes through a steady series of alterations, changing in an "indescribable way . . . that we like so much, that suits us"(62). (Actually, iDEATH is more a state of mind than a place, but I'll treat it as if it were a place, as Brautigan does for the most part.)

In Watermelon Sugar is divided into three parts of roughly equal length. In Book One we learn a bit about the narrator and his friends, and we follow him through a series of rather uneventful episodes: He walks from his shack down to iDEATH for dinner; afterwards he goes to the shack of a girl named Pauline ("my favorite," as he says[9]) and goes to bed with her; restless, he gets up in the night and goes for a long walk, a regular habit of his; in the morning he and Pauline return to iDEATH for breakfast; he then goes over to the Watermelon Works, the major industry (besides the trout hatchery, the *only* industry) in this strange community, to see his best friend, Fred; after arranging to meet Fred for lunch he returns to his shack again to work on a book he's writing. . . . The uneventfulness of these hours, we may assume, is typical of the narrator's days. As he tells us at the very beginning of his story, "I have a gentle life"(1).

Yet we also learn in Book One that the lives of the narrator and his friends were not always this gentle. In the catalogue of twenty-four things that he means to include in his book (more or less an outline of *In Watermelon Sugar*), the narrator mentions some genial, gregarious tigers that ate his parents. Soon after, we learn that there used to be lots of tigers around and that they ate many people until finally they themselves were all killed. Another ominous note in the narrator's gen-

118

erally placid list of things to include in his book is a reference to inBOIL and his gang at the Forgotten Works, "and all the terrible things they did"(9). We must wait until Book Two to find out more about this item. The third disturbing note in Book One is a whole series of references to a girl named Margaret, who was evidently the narrator's girlfriend before Pauline. Now, the narrator wants only to be free of her: "And I wish Margaret would leave me alone"(5).

Despite these disturbing references and hints, the first part of In Watermelon Sugar does move along slowly and serenely on the whole, like one of the many gentle rivers that crisscross the landscape of the novel. Even though the tigers who killed his parents twenty years ago are never far from the narrator's memory, the real keynote for Book One is the story Pauline dreams, about a lamb: "The lamb sat down in the flowers. . . . The lamb was all right" (37).

In Book Two, however, the narrator himself has a very different kind of dream. Book Two opens with the narrator returning to his shack, but instead of working on his book, he decides to take a nap. He soon falls into a dream of "again the history of inBOIL and that gang of his and the terrible things that happened just a few short months ago"(60). inBOIL, we learn, was a malcontent who "kept getting mad at things that were of no importance"(62) and who started drinking whiskey and arguing with the others at iDEATH, especially with his brother Charley (more or less the unofficial leader of iDEATH). Finally, along with some other "unhappy . . . nervous . . . shifty" men (61), he went off to the Forgotten Works, a vast scrapheap containing all the things the people of iDEATH can well do without. There, inBOIL and his followers drank whiskey and brooded over the true meaning of iDEATH, which in-BOIL had concluded was being distorted by its own inhabitants. As part of his theory, inBOIL had decided that the tigers were somehow bound up with the true meaning of iDEATH.

Finally, one terrible day, inBOIL and his drunken followers returned to show their former friends "What real iDEATH is like"(77). A ghastly orgy of self-mutilation ensued, as inBOIL and his men produced jack-knives and proceeded to cut off their own thumbs, noses, ears, fingers—until the floors of iDEATH were slippery with blood. inBOIL's last words, as he bled to death, were "I am iDEATH"(95).

Not nearly as horrified by this carnage as we might expect, the gentle inhabitants of iDEATH mopped up the blood, gathered up the bodies and severed pieces, loaded them all into wagons, and took them out to the shacks at the Forgotten Works, to burn both shacks and corpses. Just before the funeral fires were ignited, however, "Margaret came waltzing out of the Forgotten Works"(100). Margaret's fondness for the Forgotten Works—a place shunned by the other people not of inBOIL's gang—had bothered the narrator for a long time. Now, although he did not accept the prevalent suspicion "that she had conspired with inBOIL and that gang of his"(17), he felt suddenly betrayed by Margaret, and permanently alienated from her. "I could only stare at her who had disappeared into the Forgotten Works that morning"(101).

Book Three begins with the narrator waking up, feeling refreshed and oddly unaffected by his awful dream. Immediately, the leisurely, serene pace of Book One resumes. The narrator joins Fred and the community doctor, Doc Edwards, for lunch. They talk about inconsequential matters, and after lunch they part. Once again the narrator sets off for his shack to write, but, once again, he decides not to. Instead, this time, he goes down to a place called the Statue of Mirrors, where, he tells us, "Everything is reflected . . . if you stand there long enough and empty your mind of everything else but the mirrors, and you must be careful not to want anything from the mirrors"(112). He stands and watches for awhile and sees his friends going about their ordinary everyday activities—Pauline walking in the woods, Doc Edwards on his rounds, Fred busy at the Watermelon Works—but then Margaret comes into the mirror. While the narrator watches her in the Statue of Mirrors, Margaret climbs an apple tree and hangs herself from a branch.

The narrator summons Fred; together they go to break the news to Margaret's brother. The three men bring Margaret's body to iDEATH, where she is laid out properly, as if she had not become a virtual outcast. The next day Margaret is buried in the total silence that accompanies Thursday's black sun. As it is customary for the community to hold a dance after a funeral, the people reassemble at iDEATH after Margaret's burial. And the novel ends with everyone waiting for the black sun to go down so that the music can be heard.

Having laboriously summarized the main plot action of *In Watermelon Sugar*, I feel that I must certainly have confused anyone reading this book who hasn't read Brautigan's novel and maybe even those who have. What's all this about trout hatcheries and watermelons, and talking tigers and different colored suns (including a black sun that eliminates all sound)? What is the

Statue of Mirrors? Who's inBOIL? What's iDEATH? And how about the Forgotten Works? In reading *In Watermelon Sugar* we have to deal not only with a fantasy world but also with a series of idiosyncratic symbols. In order to get at the meaning of Brautigan's novel, obviously we must explore the possibilities of these symbols.

As I said earlier, *In Watermelon Sugar* seems to take place in a traumatized community, apparently after some sort of a holocaust that has led to a smash-up of a larger, more complex civilization (presumably this latter would be our present society). The people lead simple, basic lives close to the earth, evidently without such things as automobiles or electricity. The marvels of modern technology (and also books and other sophisticated cultural artifacts) have been relegated to that scrap-pile known as the Forgotten Works.

The Forgotten Works have become a kind of graveyard for unneeded, unwanted things. The names, purpose, and even nature of many of the objects heaped there have literally become forgotten. At the very beginning of *In Watermelon Sugar,* Fred shows the narrator something he's found, an object so utterly strange to him that the narrator doesn't even know how to hold it: "I tried to hold it like you would hold a flower and a rock at the same time" (7). The closest he comes to description is to say that it looks like something inBOIL and his gang might've dug up at the Forgotten Works.

But if the objects piled up in the Forgotten Works have faded or are fading from conscious memory, the Works themselves are anything but forgotten. The very existence of the towering, sinister Forgotten Works is unsettling for the narrator and his friends, as the presence of a haunted house would be for timorous children.

The works are vast, "reaching . . . into distances that we cannot travel nor want to" (69), and they go far back into time. The inscription above the gate of the Forgotten Works—"THIS IS THE ENTRANCE TO THE FORGOTTEN WORKS/BE CAREFUL/YOU MIGHT GET LOST"(69)—seems intended to recall the stern warning that Dante finds on the gates of Hell itself: "ABANDON ALL HOPE YE WHO ENTER HERE."

And the Forgotten Works are truly a Hellish place, one fatally easy to get lost in. Not only do inBOIL and his followers retreat to the Forgotten Works when they become dissatisfied with the placid life of iDEATH, but, even more significant, Margaret too gets caught up in the chaotic mysteries of the Forgotten Works, becomes virtually addicted to gathering things far better left alone. After Margaret's death, we learn that her room at iDEATH was completely filled with objects from the Forgotten Works. In contrast, besides the consistent simplicity of the other characters' lives, we have the narrator's description of his shack containing only nine things, "more or less," ranging from a child's ball to a lock of dirty hair (57–8). In so far as the Forgotten Works symbolize a kind of self-destructive materialism, Margaret can be said to have indeed gotten lost in them. And in getting lost in the Forgotten Works, she becomes a pariah.

Margaret finally belongs neither to inBOIL's suicidal gang nor to the gentle community of iDEATH. Her absence from the final showdown at iDEATH is obviously appropriate; as usual she is poking around the Forgotten Works. Although the narrator does not believe that Margaret is a conscious traitor to iDEATH, clearly he does come to consider her an alien creature; in his very first reference to Margaret, he calls her "they"(3), that pronoun so often used to designate an unknown, anonymous, almost impersonal enemy. Also, in the same short chapter, he refers to her annoying habit of invariably stepping on the one loose board on the bridge to his shack; since no one else ever steps on the loose board, Margaret's habit is another indication of her alien otherness. Much later in the novel, the narrator tells us that when he was in love with Margaret her step on that board "pleased me and made my stomach tingle like a bell set ajar"(65). Margaret's obsession with the sinister Forgotten Works loses her the narrator's love and the friendship of the community. She can only resolve her dilemma by choosing inBOIL's way, the way of death.

Besides serving as Margaret's ultimate mentor by preceding her to the Forgotten Works and to suicide, inBOIL also provides a connection between the Forgotten Works and the other nightmarish symbol in *In Watermelon Sugar*. After moving to a shack at the Forgotten Works, inBOIL is heard to say "something about the tigers being a good deal"(76). The tigers of course are all dead and have been for years, but like the Forgotten Works they remain as a strong negative psychological force. The narrator says at one point, "It had taken years to get over the tigers and the terrible things they had done to us"(75), but by the disturbing tenacity of his memory of the tigers, the narrator makes it very clear that he at least has not really "gotten over" them. The tigers devoured the narrator's parents before his eyes, while chatting amiably with him, a fact that is never far from his mind, even though it happened twenty years before the time of the novel. The tigers were terrible predators who had to be ruthlessly exterminated, and were.

And yet the tigers were also beautiful creatures, with

pleasant voices, who were polite and friendly to children and some grownups. Not only did they chat with the narrator while they ate his parents, but they offered to tell him a story and they helped him with his arithmetic homework. When the last tiger was killed, the narrator tells us, the people threw flowers on its funeral pyre "and stood around crying because it was the last tiger"(31). The tigers were killed only with reluctance and with the recognition that, as Charley says, "they can't help themselves..."(35). Among the numerous statues and lanterns in the world of *In Watermelon Sugar* are several of each in the form of tigers.

A friend of mine has suggested to me that Brautigan's tigers might be modelled after the tiger of William Blake's great poem. Whether Brautigan had Blake consciously in mind when writing *In Watermelon Sugar* I don't know,[2] but I do think that his tigers, like Blake's tiger, are intended to function as symbols of unbridled energy. More explicitly, I think that Brautigan means the tigers to represent a kind of self-destructive aggression that generally comes with adulthood (as I've said, the tigers never harmed children, respecting, as it were, the Blakean state of Innocence). Significantly, we are told early in the novel of Charley's theory that "maybe we were tigers a long time ago"(31). Killing the tigers, then, can be seen as a necessary but painful purging of aggressive instincts from men themselves, as an elimination of the tiger-ness that comes with maturity.

When inBOIL returns to iDEATH for his suicidal confrontation with Charley and the others, he says, "The tigers should never have been killed. The tigers were the true meaning of iDEATH"(93). iDEATH is the central thematic symbol of *In Watermelon Sugar*, and inBOIL's perverted association of the tigers and

125

iDEATH helps us obliquely to get at the "true meaning" of iDEATH. Or, rather, meanings, for this complex symbol functions in several ways.

Most obviously and probably most importantly, iDEATH represents the-death-of-the-I (appropriately lower-cased by Brautigan to show the proper insignificance of this pronoun), or the death of the aggressive, ambitious, ego. Living in or near iDEATH (as I've already suggested, iDEATH is symbolically more a state of mind than a place), the members of the community are without the driving egoistic needs; they live as placidly as trout, without rank, status, money, laws or any of the other imperatives of the ego. Free from these things (the tigers dead, the Forgotten Works fading), the inhabitants of iDEATH concern themselves only with the simple elemental things of life and attune themselves to the primal rhythms of Nature. They perhaps can reach the condition described by R. D. Laing in his account of the man who passed through schizophrenia to a state of inner peace: "He had not died physically, but his 'ego' had died. Along with this ego-loss, this death, came feelings of the enhanced significance and relevance of everything."[3] Perhaps they can even approach that transcendent state celebrated by Blake, in *A Song of Liberty* (as well as in other poems), in which "Everything that Lives is Holy!"

A second important meaning of iDEATH, coexisting with its primary meaning, is death-of-idea (idea/death), in the sense of the death of abstract ideas, theories, ideologies, concepts. In this respect, *In Watermelon Sugar* may be compared to works by such twentieth-century writers as Hermann Hesse and Kurt Vonnegut, both of whom, like Brautigan, show mistrust or sometimes hostility toward excessive reliance on reason or even thought. To choose brief examples from the best-known books of each of these authors, one of the chief things the protagonist of Hesse's *Siddhartha* has to learn is to reject abstract formalized knowledge for concrete experience; Bokonon, the philosopher in Vonnegut's *Cat's Cradle,* prefaces his book with a warning to the reader to close the book at once, for it is nothing but lies. Similarly, in *In Watermelon Sugar,* books have been generally relegated to the Forgotten Works; their main purpose is as winter fuel.

Books are still written occasionally, of course—the narrator, as I've said, is engaged in writing one—but, we're told, only twenty-four books have been written in 171 years, and "The last one was written thirty-five years ago"(9). And, although the narrator is certainly not an outcast, as Margaret becomes, he *is* something of an outsider or loner. It's perhaps significant that when the narrator goes up to iDEATH for the first time in the novel, Pauline's greeting is "Hi, stranger" (17). The narrator, as I've said, does not have a regular name and is in the habit of taking long walks. He also spends more time in his shack—away from iDEATH—than any of his friends. It might be said that his need to write comes from his relative inability to lose himself thoughtlessly in the flow of experience. Paradoxically, his very restlessness (symbolized by his changing names as much as by his walks) keeps him from fully discovering/losing himself in iDEATH.

There is one other meaning of iDEATH that has to be considered: the perverted interpretation of iDEATH by inBOIL. Where the narrator is mildly restless, inBOIL suffers from a ferocious internal ferment; as his name suggests, he is boiling within. inBOIL is a man who is unable to accept the noncompetitive, aggressionless, status-less world of iDEATH. Blake said that "Energy is Eternal Delight" (*Marriage of Heaven and Hell*), but in his gruesome depiction of inBOIL Brautigan seems to raise the question of the sinister potential of misdirected energy. The implicit question raised by inBOIL's role in *In Watermelon Sugar* is similar to that posed by Theodore Roszak in his discussion of nihilistic tendencies in current American counter culture: "How is one to make certain that the exploration of the non-intellective powers will not degenerate into a maniacal nihilism?"[4]

Driven by the same sort of furious energy as the tigers, with which he finally identifies, inBOIL attempts to negate the negation of the ego. Instead of iDEATH as the-death-of-the-I, he comes to see it as the ultimate manifestation of the *I*. The tigers were the true meaning of iDEATH and a "good deal" for inBOIL because they were *all* aggression, all ego, all will, rather than the negation of these things. Like Kirilov in Dostoevsky's *The Devils*, inBOIL tries to assert his will and identity in what Roszak might consider an ultimate act of "maniacal nihilism," by committing suicide. Drunk at least as much with a sense of power as with whiskey, inBOIL literally cuts off his nose to spite his face, hacks off pieces of him*self* to assert his *self*hood. In response to inBOIL's dying declaration that he is/has become iDEATH, Pauline—busy with mop and bucket as she cleans up the blood of inBOIL and his followers—very sensibly replies, "You're an asshole"(95).

In inBOIL, Margaret, and the narrator, Brautigan gives us three characters who, in different ways and to different degrees, are unable to lose themselves in the will-less, mindless harmonious peace of iDEATH. (In some respects, Pauline might appear to be a fourth outsider, for we learn that she was "the girl with the lantern" whom the narrator used to see on his lonely walks. But when she finds love she becomes much less restless and as internally secure as any of the characters in the novel; instead of taking long solitary walks, she dreams of lambs.) inBOIL is the frustrated leader who is only able to develop his aggressive, egoistic instincts along self-destructive lines. Margaret, on the other hand, is a person who is unable to give up her acquisitive drives and gets lost in the wilderness of her own senseless materialism. The narrator is a portrait of the artist in a world where art as the expression of one's ego has ceased to be relevant because the people have purged themselves of ego.

Even though he himself is a writer of books and obviously somewhat bookish, Brautigan's attitude toward books and literature is in general somewhat negative throughout his work. At best, his attitude toward books can be seen as ambivalent; at worst, it is virtually hostile. In *The Abortion,* of course, the books written by the numerous people who come to the library for losers are mostly direct projections of their loneliness, frustrations, or obsessions. The library itself is a kind of Forgotten Works where the books are stored never to be read by anyone. The only "value" of these books is as a kind of self-therapy: Vida writing down the hatred she feels toward her own luscious body; the teenage boy relating the agonies of his sexual awakening; saddest of all, the doctor's neatly typed 300-page call for legalized abortion, which no one will ever read ("There's nothing else I can do" [*Abortion,* p. 32]). Except for the books written by the very young (*My Trike* by Chuck), the very old—always a favorite group in Brautigan (*Grow-*

129

ing Flowers by Candlelight in Hotel Rooms by Mrs. Charles Fine Adams)—and other simple, uncomplicated people *(Hombre,* a Western, by a retired Chinese cook), the books that come to the library in *The Abortion* are sad or even pathetic expressions of the egos of their authors.

In the world of *In Watermelon Sugar,* there is little need for this kind of ego-expression. The major art form (almost the only art form) is sculpture. The statues mentioned in the novel are mostly either celebrations of simple, pleasant, common things (crickets, trout, vegetables) or commemorations of things gone but not forgotten (tigers, friends or loved ones—e.g., the narrator's statue of his mother, which he refers to several times). In my imagination, the statues resemble the directly representational form of that famous "Alice in Wonderland" statue in New York's Central Park, beloved by hippies, or the statue of Benjamin Franklin in San Francisco's Washington Square, which Brautigan uses so affectionately on the cover and elsewhere in *Trout Fishing in America.* Aside from subject matter and intent (celebration or commemoration), the other important thing about the statues in *In Watermelon Sugar* is that they are unsigned, anonymous. Again, this is obviously appropriate to the iDEATH state of mind, to the extinction of the ego; the emphasis in the statues is on the created object, not at all on the creator.

The narrator's friends are really neither interested in writing nor reading books. Accepting but not sharing his need for self-expression, they ask about his book-in-progress politely from time to time. They know that certain people have a need to write books, even if they can't understand why. Charley tells the narrator that the last man who wrote a book, thirty-five years ago, was like the narrator in that "He didn't have a regular name"(10). Aside from Pauline, who loves him, and the schoolteacher, who has an amusing pride in an old pupil making good, no one shows more than mild curiosity about the narrator's book. In iDEATH the people lead their gentle orderly lives without need of books, almost without need of thought. They are concerned with simple things, not fancy words; one day out of seven—during the soundless black sun's duration—they have no words, and they get along all right, as Margaret's funeral shows. Perhaps the best comment on the place of books in the world of *In Watermelon Sugar* comes from one of the seed-packet poems ("Sweet Alyssum Royal Carpet") in Brautigan's *Please Plant This Book:*

> I've decided to live in a world where
> books are changed into thousands
> of gardens with children playing
> in the gardens and learning the gen-
> tle ways of green growing things.

The 375 people of iDEATH have repudiated the culture and technology of our complex civilization, have relegated modern "accomplishments" to the Forgotten Works. For these things, they have substituted "the gentle ways of green growing things." The world of *In Watermelon Sugar* is an edenic place filled with what we may assume to be items that carry personal value and meaning for Brautigan: watermelons, rivers, trout, woods, bridges. . . . There are rivers everywhere, some of them only a few inches wide, for, as the narrator says, "We call everything a river here"(2). The rivers are all well-stocked with trout, Brautigan's favorite and most famous symbol. Bridges—made of wood, stone, or even watermelon sugar—straddle the rivers. And, in between rivers, the landscape alternates between piney woods and watermelon fields.

And from the watermelons comes the juice that is made into the sugar that is the stuff of the lives and dreams of the people of iDEATH: "We take the juice from the watermelons and cook it down until there's nothing left but sugar, and then we work it into the shape of this thing that we have: our lives"(33). The title of the novel, of course, is *In Watermelon Sugar;* the title of Book One is also "In Watermelon Sugar"; the first chapter is called "In Watermelon Sugar"; the book begins, "In watermelon sugar . . ."; the first sentence of the book ends, ". . . in watermelon sugar." Throughout the novel, the phrase recurs, like a refrain. The whole novel is steeped, drenched (some might even say drowned) in watermelon sugar, in, that is to say, the distillation of the central object among which the characters lead their simple elemental lives. (It should be noted that trout oil is also an important product in *In Watermelon Sugar,* but I'll save my remarks on Brautigan and trout for my discussion of *Trout Fishing in America.*) Having discarded the so-called marvels of modern civilization, the gentle souls of iDEATH have, almost literally, reduced (or boiled down) their lives to basic essentials, symbolized by the "sweet and gentle" watermelon sugar.

Brautigan's repeated use of the phrase, "in watermelon sugar," emphasizes the integration of the characters' lives with the world of Nature. In writing his novel this way, Brautigan might be said to be heeding one of his own poems, again from *Please Plant This Book* ("Squash"):

> the time is right to mix sentences with
> dirt and the sun with punctuation
> and the rain with verbs. . . .

(I am aware, incidentally, that some people like to read *In Watermelon Sugar* as a kind of acid allegory, to see iDEATH as a drug-induced state of heightened (or anyway altered) consciousness and "watermelon sugar" as a euphemism for LSD or some other hallucinogen (a Brautiganian equivalent of Ken Kesey's electric kool-aid). I suppose there's no harm in this approach, but it doesn't take you very far; it takes you to the beginning of what *In Watermelon Sugar* is about, not to the end.)

The world of *In Watermelon Sugar* is both constantly changing and always the same. As I've said, there is a different colored sun every day, which in turn leads to different colored watermelons, but the sun changes in a coherent predictable pattern: red on Monday, golden on Tuesday, and so forth. Like the sunshine, rainfall varies but is predictable. We are told at one point that "The first rain of the year would not start until the 12th day of October"(44). Similarly, iDEATH constantly changes in form and shape, but its changes are also recurrent, and, in addition, in all of its many forms it is warm and cheery. (Near the end of the novel, the narrator says that iDEATH does have "lasting forms" (120), perhaps signifying that its qualities (as opposed to its externals) are permanent—warmth, cheeriness, hospitality—that it is always a "good place"[8].)

This pattern of variety within uniformity has its parallel in the very ceremonious, almost ritualized lives the characters lead. The one cafe near iDEATH serves a different lunch on each day of the week, but the same meal on the same day of each week. The waitress who presides over this regular pattern of meals has been at the cafe "for years"(107). As the funeral following Margaret's death makes clear, despite the lack of formalized rules and regulations (these, presumably, belong in the Forgotten Works), nearly everything that occurs in iDEATH is governed by custom: "It's our custom," says Charley, "to brick up the rooms of those who have lived here when they die"(124). Later the narrator informs us that "It is a custom here to hold a dance in the trout hatchery after a funeral"(130).

The important opening sentence of *In Watermelon Sugar*, it seems to me, can best be understood in relation to the ritualized aspect of life in iDEATH: "In watermelon sugar the deeds were done and done again as my life is done in watermelon sugar"(1). The key words here are "the deeds were done and done again," implying a recurrence, a pattern, a rhythm; this sense of recurrence is emphasized by the repetition of the opening phrase at the end of the first sentence. The anxiety caused by inBOIL's insurrection against iDEATH (if insurrection is the word) recurs in the narrator's dream of this episode, but so does the relief from this anxiety which followed, which is also part of the dream. Presumably Margaret's suicide will likewise recur in subsequent dreams, but so will the recovery of harmony in the dance that follows her funeral. It might even be said that the narrator's having witnessed Margaret's suicide in the Statue of Mirrors is part of the rhythm of iDEATH. Evidently, due to her estrangement from iDEATH, Margaret's death by suicide has become inevitable. "It was nobody's fault," the narrator assures Pauline. "Just one of those things" (122).

For all of the genial anarchism of iDEATH, it is a very conservative society, evidently governed by a strong

134

collective need for order. The narrator tells us with obvious approval that in Pauline's shack "Everything was in its proper order"(28), a contrast, as we later learn, to Margaret's disorderly room crowded with dangerous relics of the Forgotten Works. At one point, the narrator pauses in his narrative to comment pleasurably on a bridge in which all the stones have been "placed in their proper order"(74). Similarly—and significantly— he tells us that watermelon sugar, trout juice, and herbs are mixed together "in their proper time to make this fine oil that we use to light our world"(83). Just about everything in iDEATH is in its proper place; everything is done in its proper time.

The heavy emphasis on custom, ceremony, and order throughout *In Watermelon Sugar* strongly reinforces the implicit sense of a post-holocaust, traumatized world. One of the important questions raised by Brautigan's novel was asked fifty years ago by W. B. Yeats, in his poem "A Prayer for My Daughter": "How but in custom and ceremony/Are innocence and beauty born?"[5] In another poem—one of the most famous poems of the twentieth century—Yeats expresses what might be considered a keynote for *In Watermelon Sugar* (as well as for many other literary works of the last fifty years): "Things fall apart; the centre cannot hold."[6] The world of Brautigan's novel is one in which things have fallen apart, in which the center has not held, in which too (to juggle Yeats' words in the same poem) the "ceremony of innocence" has been and still is threatened by imminent drowning. It is a world in which the characters of iDEATH have fashioned a small, simple, modest, coherent, controlled life-style, thereby regaining "innocence and beauty." If, as I've argued, the tigers and the Forgotten Works both symbolize destructive aspects

135

of our present culture, then the world of iDEATH clearly represents a fantasy version of the counter culture, in which these destructive things have been banished.

On the first page of *In Watermelon Sugar*, the narrator says, "there is a delicate balance in iDEATH." And so there is. The narrator seems to be chiefly referring to the balance of rhythm of time and the seasons that the inhabitants of iDEATH have attuned themselves to and to the gentle lives they lead in harmony with Nature's "green growing things." Life and death are, of course, part of this cycle, and thus are accepted by the characters without much fuss. Shortly before Margaret commits suicide, Doc Edwards delivers a new baby (a girl) into the small community, an obvious indication of the recurrence of life. Even more significant is the custom of holding a dance—a celebration of life, as it were—after a funeral. The novel ends with the musicians "poised with their instruments"(138) and the dancers, dressed in their modest best and "in fairly good spirits"(138), ready to go. The fact that the dance is to be held in the trout hatchery at iDEATH is important too, for we learn that the trout hatchery was built upon the site where the last tiger was killed—out of the death of the ferocious destructive tigers, the gentle fecund trout.

But there is another and less optimistic way in which the characters of *In Watermelon Sugar* may be said to live in "a delicate balance." This novel is not only less humorous than Brautigan's other books (unless we consider gentle whimsy as humor, which I don't), it is also considerably more subdued. It has really none of the boisterous exuberance provided by characters like Foster (in *The Abortion*) and Lee Mellon (in *Confed-*

erate General). Virtually the only character in *In Water-melon Sugar* who shows passion or even enthusiasm is inBOIL, the closest thing to a villain in all of Brauti-gan's work. It's significant that inBOIL should be the most passionate character in the novel, and it's appropri-ate that he should be identified with whiskey, so much so that his slovenly deterioration is partly attributed to his drinking. In Brautigan's other books, whiskey and wine are generally treated positively, as good things—Foster's arrival at the library with bourbon, the various cheerful drinking episodes in *Confederate General* and *Trout Fishing in America,* the affectionate description of the narrator's grandmother's bootlegging career in "Revenge of the Lawn," references in poems like "The Winos on Portrero Hill." But in *In Watermelon Sugar,* surprisingly, whiskey is treated with what can only be called puritanical condemnation.

Whiskey, supposedly, inflames a person's passions or emotions, and one important and somewhat depress-ing aspect of iDEATH is the curious lack of emotion there. As I've said, the survivors exhibit little reaction to the gory suicides of inBOIL and his gang. Even Margaret's death does not evoke much emotion; her brother when told of her suicide, seems to grieve silently for "a little while" but then quickly concludes, "It's for the best"(118). The narrator's tone is subdued through-out; even in his relationships with Margaret and Pauline he shows affection more than passion. Aside from in-BOIL, the only important character who shows much emotion in fact (anger towards inBOIL, grief toward the death of Margaret) is Pauline, and she, as I've said, is or at one time was at least partly an outsider, the girl with the lantern whom the narrator used to see on his own lonely walks. *Her* walks might have been a result of her inability to subdue her emotions.

This lack of passion or emotion is obviously an important point in *In Watermelon Sugar*. As much as *The Abortion* or *Confederate General*, this novel deals with the question of dominating or controlling one's world. Unlike the other two novels, however, *In Watermelon Sugar* gives us a world in which the characters can cope with their lives. But to do this they have not only stripped their lives down to simple essentials and attuned themselves to the basic rhythms of life, they have also had to subdue or even eliminate strong feelings. For in the world of Brautigan's novel passion may lead to getting lost in the Forgotten Works or to a rejuvenation of the tigers.

"I hope this works out," the narrator says, on the very first page of *In Watermelon Sugar*. "This" presumably refers to his narrative, to the book itself, the book he is writing "one word after another"(107), instead of making statues. In a sense, of course, the book is the narrator's statue, celebrating the delicate balance of iDEATH. *In Watermelon Sugar* is directly addressed to those of us who are still living among the Forgotten Works and who are still ravaged by tigers—"because I am here and you are distant"(1). The novel ends at the moment just before the black silent sun goes down, when harmony and order will be restored and the affirmative dance of life will recommence. When we have travelled the length of the narrator's life and dreams, his book—his monument to iDEATH—is complete. The last sentence of *In Watermelon Sugar* emphasizes this sense of a finished job, of deeds done and done again: "It would only be a few seconds now, I wrote"(138).

Some of Brautigan's critics have felt strongly that *In Watermelon Sugar* does not "work out." Thomas Lask, for instance, asserts that the novel is a "feeble and amateurish exercise. It took 30 minutes to read and seemed interminable."[7] A more sympathetic critic, the novelist, Thomas McGuane, has ambivalent feelings about *In Watermelon Sugar*. He finds it a "relentlessly enigmatic, even ethereal novel."[8] Although for me *In Watermelon Sugar* succeeds as a whole better than either *The Abortion* or even *Confederate General* (perhaps because it takes me more than 30 minutes to read?), I do think that the book presents a couple of major problems.

First of all, Brautigan faces the same basic difficulty in this novel as in *The Abortion*: a deficiency, for much of the book, of intrinsic dramatic interest. As McGuane says, *In Watermelon Sugar* "is concrete to the point of studied anti-selectivity. Through whole pages people talk assiduously of nothing whatever." Again as in *The Abortion*, I believe that this general lack of dramatic material can be justified. Obviously an account of simple, gentle people leading placid lives has to be pretty low-keyed. Moreover, the placidity of Book One makes a very effective contrast to the nightmarish violence of Book Two, the section dealing with the horrible suicides of inBOIL and his followers. Nevertheless, surely Brautigan runs the risk of simply boring his readers in chapters like "Meat Loaf" and "Apple Pie"(106–9), the main business of which is a discussion among the narrator, Fred, and Doc Edwards about what they want for lunch. In one way, the anti-dramatic material is more of a problem in *In Watermelon Sugar* than in *The Abortion* because in the latter even the most inconsequential pas-

139

sages (e.g., a conversation between the narrator and Vida in an airport restaurant) might afford amusing insights into American society, while the former, being a fantasy, cannot make direct comments of this kind. On the other hand, however, the fact that *In Watermelon Sugar is* fantasy suggests that even the most commonplace details will have some interest, since we're trying to size up a strange, new world. Also *In Watermelon Sugar* is only about half as long as *The Abortion,* so perhaps Brautigan only has to worry half as much about the reader getting bogged down in real or apparent trivia.

A second problem a reader might have in responding to *In Watermelon Sugar* is Brautigan's presentation of the details of the strange world of iDEATH. There's a thin line between a set of symbols so open (or "enigmatic," to use McGuane's term) as to be arbitrary and so fixed as to be mechanical or rigid. To be really effective, it seems to me, a fable has to somehow avoid falling over either side of this line. For me personally the only symbol in *In Watermelon Sugar* that doesn't work particularly well is the Statue of Mirrors. It can be explained, I guess ("justified"), in terms of the controlled predictability of life in iDEATH, but I still find the Statue of Mirrors kind of gimmicky and mechanical, like something Brautigan might have thought of and brought in at the last minute. Aside from the Statue of Mirrors, however, it seems to me that Brautigan has done a wonderful job of creating a fantasy world that is complete in its own terms and yet has relevance to the real world. In managing this he has achieved a meaningful fable for our times, these bad times in which we are all wandering in the Forgotten Works of materialism and menaced by the tigers of aggression.

Although *In Watermelon Sugar* is Brautigan's most

140

original book—a novel quite unlike any other the reader is liable to encounter in plot, setting, and style[9]—it is, as I've said, related thematically to his other works, as well as to other important contemporary American books. In a sense, *In Watermelon Sugar* might be described as a fantasy extension of *The Abortion* and *Confederate General.* Where *The Abortion* shows us two small people trying to cope within the limits of "gentle necessity" and *Confederate General* shows us a group of characters comically trying to assert their dominance of "this shit pile," *In Watermelon Sugar* presents a world scaled down to dimensions with which the characters can cope. That Brautigan's brave new world is not the simple-minded paradise some of his critics have assumed it to be is made clear not only by the ghastly examples of inBOIL and Margaret, but also by the subdued and determinedly unemotional tone of the book.

In Watermelon Sugar has an interesting relationship to that recent best seller, Charles Reich's *The Greening of America* (1970). Although Reich never mentions Brautigan, perhaps hasn't read him, his definition of Consciousness III is quite like the state of iDEATH. In Consciousness III, says Reich, "the individual frees himself from automatic acceptance of the imperatives of society and the false consciousness which society imposes."[10] The repudiation of the Forgotten Works in Brautigan's novel is surely a rejection of the "false consciousness" Reich is talking about. Indeed, Reich's assertion that "man must create his own fictions and live by them"[11] reads almost like a description of Brautigan's method in *In Watermelon Sugar.*

A book even closer in spirit to *In Watermelon Sugar* than *The Greening of America* (and also, I think, a much better book) is Raymond Mungo's *Total Loss*

Farm(1970). Mungo presumably has read Brautigan (for one thing, he uses the term "iDEATH" several times), and his formulation of the motto of Total Loss Farm could serve as a motto for the true meaning of iDEATH: "Total Loss Farm: lose yourself."[12] Significantly, Mungo refers to the people living on Total Loss Farm as "children" throughout, which parallels Brautigan's depiction of iDEATH as a state of innocence regained (which is to say that both Total Loss Farm and iDEATH are regressive states, in so-called normal terms). Moreover, Mungo's account of how the communal farm came into being reads like a real-life equivalent of the origins of Brautigan's fantasy world: "Total Loss Farm . . . was born when the outer society became such a bore, and descended into such thorough decay, they said 'fuck it' and went off to live in a world not yet of human making and see if they couldn't do better."[13]

Brautigan's fictive world too is one in which the characters have gone off to see if they can't do better. "Wherever you are," says the narrator on the first page of *In Watermelon Sugar*, "we must do the best we can." This statement is surely the thematic center of this novel and perhaps the central statement of Brautigan's work as a whole. Those critics who see Brautigan as a gentle, amiable imbecile would probably say that the statement sums up all that he has to say. But of course it does not. In *In Watermelon Sugar*, Brautigan shows us that coping with one's life requires strength and a complex act of will. The triumph of the novel, it seems to me, is the way Brautigan diagrams what the narrator calls (in reference to Pauline), "strength gained through the process of gentleness"(21).

Chapter Six.
Toward a Vision of America:
Trout Fishing in America

Coming finally to Brautigan's most famous and most
acclaimed book, I find myself confronted by a formi-
dable problem that doesn't exist in his other three novels.
Unlike *The Abortion, A Confederate General from Big
Sur,* and *In Watermelon Sugar, Trout Fishing in America*
(1967) does not have a continuous, clearly defined narrative line for the reader to follow or hang on to. The
book consists of forty-seven brief chapters or episodes
(ranging from about half a page to six pages in length)

covering a wide variety of subjects.[1] Most of the chapters are not in fact explicitly about trout fishing; some don't have much to do with any recognizable American reality; a few (such as "Another Method of Making Walnut Catsup") don't seem to have much to do with anything. To say that *Trout Fishing in America* is loosely organized would be to understate wildly. The book appears to have no real principle of organization at all. At first reading (and probably at second or even third), it might seem as if the chapters could be reshuffled arbitrarily without violation of the structure of the book.

The obvious temptation is to approach *Trout Fishing in America* as if it were a formless miscellany and to write a series of discursive comments as loosely organized as Brautigan's book itself. This approach would seem to receive support from the fact that Brautigan has said that he lost two chapters before the original publication of *Trout Fishing in America;* their separate publication several years later in *Esquire* (October 1970) implies that the entire idea of talking about the book as a more or less coherent whole is preposterous.

I might get around the problem of the structure of *Trout Fishing in America* by organizing my discussion along similar lines to my earlier chapter on *Revenge of the Lawn.* I might focus on the episodes that seem most striking or significant, without worrying too much about which episode precedes which, or about the relationship between episodes. Such an approach would at least have the negative merit of keeping me from imposing an artificial or mechanical order on the book. "Beware of the structure freak," as a Yippie is supposed to have said in Chicago during the terrible summer of 1968.[2]

One of Brautigan's most sympathetic critics, Robert Adams, has argued that none of Brautigan's extended prose works can properly be considered a novel. Although he says that *Trout Fishing in America* is the most "diffuse and episodic" of the novels, he suggests that all four "may well go down in literary history as Brautigans"[3]—that is to say, as books that can only be approached on their own terms, within their own tiny separate category. Another perceptive critic of *Trout Fishing in America,* John Clayton, asserts that "the book runs profoundly counter to the bourgeois instincts of the novel" and that it should be considered neither a novel nor even an anti-novel but rather what Clayton calls an "un-novel."[4]

And yet, in his quiet way, Brautigan seems insistent that *Trout Fishing in America* is a novel after all. Not only was the book labelled as such when originally published, but in the short story "Forgiven," Brautigan makes reference to "a novel called *Trout Fishing in America*" (*Revenge of the Lawn,* 165). Whether we designate the book a "novel" or an "un-novel," a "Brautigan" or just a "book" is of course not the important point. It does seem to me, though, that it is important to consider the shape and form of *Trout Fishing in America,* to see where the book goes and how it gets there. To write a series of miscellaneous notes on Brautigan's miscellaneous episodes would be to compete with the author rather than to illuminate his book. More important, as I've already said several times in this study, Brautigan's critics in general, even the sympathetic ones, tend to condescend to his books, to treat them as amiable, trivial, empty little entertainments.[5] I think that *Trout Fishing in America,* like Brautigan's other novels, can stand up to critical analysis.

There are obvious risks involved in looking for structural coherence (for pattern, for overall organization) in a book as diffuse and profuse as *Trout Fishing in America*. Again, beware of the structure freak. In my discussion, I'll try to avoid, on the one hand, distorting the book to make it fit into an imposed order, and, on the other, pretending that the episodes that don't quite fit in aren't in the novel at all. I do believe that *Trout Fishing in America* does hold together, more or less; that we can get more out of the book by seeing it as a whole, as a novel. However, I also have to admit that there are some episodes that don't really seem to fit into the overall structure of the book, some places where, as John Lennon might say, Brautigan appears to have been just sticking things in. I must preface my discussion of the structure of *Trout Fishing in America* by noting how in that book the narrator tells us of once getting caught up in the mystery of a cat with the improbable name "208." The mystery seemed unsolvable: why would anyone name a cat 208? "I thought about it for a while," says the narrator, "hiding it from the rest of my mind. But I didn't ruin my birthday by secretly thinking about it too hard"(69).

The first and most obvious thing to say about the structure of *Trout Fishing in America* is that the book *does* have a fairly well defined beginning, middle, and end. Although the episodes move around in time a good deal (for instance, there are several flashbacks to the narrator's childhood), the central chapters (those actually pertaining to trout fishing and/or camping) are all set within a period of about a year—beginning at a point shortly before the narrator's daughter is born. The narrator, his "woman" (as he calls her throughout), and their baby daughter roam the American West, fishing,

146

camping, exploring—looking for a quiet, simple pastoral existence. Indeed, they might be described as three characters in search of a pastoral myth. The last third of *Trout Fishing in America* is crowded with episodes emphasizing in different ways the disappearance or commercialization of the great American outdoors: the narrator's conversation with the disgruntled doctor who searches in vain for the old America; the story of Mr. Norris, who loads himself down with camping equipment only to find the campgrounds all filled up with people; the narrator's climactic final meeting with that mythic figure, Trout Fishing in America; the crucial account of the Cleveland Wrecking Yard, with its trout streams for sale by the foot; the narrator's brief meditation on Leonardo da Vinci, reincarnated as an American designer of commercial fishing lures which receive endorsements from "Thirty-four ex-presidents of the United States" (108). Finally, the narrator and his small family give up their nomadic existence and settle with friends in a cabin in California. The chapter following "The Last Time I Saw Trout Fishing in America" begins, "I've come home from Trout Fishing in America . . ." (92).

Even on the most superficial level, we can see a kind of thematic development in *Trout Fishing in America*. A young man and his family try to live with absolute freedom and independence, only to realize that such a way of life is no longer possible in America, if it ever was. Once again, as in *A Confederate General from Big Sur*, Brautigan is writing in a rich American tradition, expressing that need for freedom from social confinements that runs through such writers as Thoreau and Mark Twain; once again, unlike his predecessors in American Pastoral, Brautigan includes a woman (and

147

even a child) in his protagonist's flight from society.

If the central episodes of *Trout Fishing in America* follow a chronological sequence (roughly from the Fall of 1960 through the Fall of 1961), it is still true, as I said before, that these trout fishing episodes account for only a relatively small part of the book, about one-third of the forty-seven chapters. Obviously, the question to be asked at this point is, What about the rest of the book? John Clayton points out that the "freedom and rambling" theme in *Trout Fishing in America* is paralleled by the apparent disorder of the book. "It isn't true that the parts of *Trout Fishing in America* could be shuffled at random . . . but we are intended to *feel* that there is absolutely no ordering."[6] This precarious balance between order and disorder is achieved, I think, by Brautigan's audacious narrative method.

Speaking broadly, the method of narration in *Trout Fishing in America* can be described as stream of consciousness. (Perhaps a more apt phrase would be trout stream of consciousness.[7]) Throughout the novel, the episodes which seem unrelated to the central movement of the book—the attempt by the narrator to resist "the fickle wind of the Twentieth Century"(92)—can be seen as associative memories and meditations or as imaginative fantasies which amplify the surface theme. This flow of memories, meditations, and fantasies does have a direct relationship to what I have been calling the central narrative movement of *Trout Fishing in America*. The relationship is not always (or even usually) apparent at first because Brautigan has left out the sort of transitions or connectives that we're accustomed to in reading a conventional novel. Brautigan's method is more like what we'd expect in a long twentieth-century poem, rather than in a novel. William Carlos Williams' great poem, *Patterson*—with its constant interplay between past and present, with its vibration between the specific and personal and the general and universal—is perhaps as close in structure to *Trout Fishing in America* as any contemporary work, though there are parallels in such famous poems as T.S. Eliot's *Wasteland* and Ezra Pound's *Cantos* too.

But in order to get at the implicit structure of *Trout Fishing in America* it is necessary to first discuss the major symbol in the book, the actual phrase, "Trout Fishing in America."[8] The implications of that term are at least as elusive as the significance of "in watermelon sugar," and they are even more critical to Brautigan's meaning. Although the categories overlap and at times the symbol functions in more than one way, in general there are five separate aspects to Brautigan's title phrase. First and most obviously, trout fishing in America means just what the words say—the experience of fishing for trout in America. This obvious dimension should not be overlooked, for there is no question but that Brautigan seriously believes—like Hemingway—in the curative, almost sacramental, value of fishing, that, as in the short story, "Forgiven," fishing can provide answers to "complicated questions" (*Revenge of the Lawn*, 165). Or, as one character says in *Trout Fishing in America*, that "Trout fishing is one of the best things in the world . . ."(73).

But Trout Fishing in America is also a place—call it the Great Outdoors, the Wilderness, or Nature. When the narrator says, "I've come home from Trout Fishing in America," he chiefly means that he has settled for the relative restrictions of life in his friend's rented cabin, in contrast to the unsuccessful attempt at a life of total freedom. A third and more important sense of

149

the title phrase is the idea of Trout Fishing in America as more than a literal place—as, rather, a state of mind, or what Clayton calls "a mental space . . . where we can all live in freedom."[9] In this sense, Trout Fishing in America is quite like the state of iDEATH in *In Watermelon Sugar;* it is any place where people can be said to have "a good world going for them"(69). Significantly, the two people who are described as having found this "good world"—an ex-convict and a former whore—live in a run-down hotel called Hotel Trout Fishing in America.

Trout Fishing in America is a character, a person too. A person who walks and talks and receives letters and even signs his name. In the narrator's imagination, Trout Fishing in America dines with Maria Callas; he remembers Lewis and Clark; he seems to have strangely inappropriate disciples—Jack the Ripper and a legless, malevolent "evil fart" known as Trout Fishing in America Shorty.

Finally and most significantly, embracing and transcending all of the other aspects of the phrase, Trout Fishing in America is a kind of spirit, a mythic quality that serves to unite various apparently disparate elements in the book. Ultimately, Jack the Ripper and Trout Fishing in America Shorty are *not* the true disciples of Trout Fishing in America; instead they are perverted or degraded manifestations of what has happened to the pastoral myth of America as a land of freedom. The real heirs of Trout Fishing in America are those schoolboys who resist the stultifying indoctrination of the classroom by chalking "Trout Fishing in America" on the backs of first-graders, those "Trout Fishing in America Terrorists"(37), and that older but parallel group, the protesting "communist" demonstrators, who

"Witness for Trout Fishing in America Peace"(98). Brautigan is surely not, as one critic asserts, "crazy with optimism" in *Trout Fishing in America.*[10] Rather, he imagines an instinctive conspiracy or counter culture made up of all those who resist the present realities of American life. The numerous American outlaws or criminals evoked in the novel—John Dillinger, Billy the Kid, Pretty Boy Floyd, even Caryl Chessman—are part of the Trout Fishing in America conspiracy. So is Richard Lawrence Marquette, the "avid trout fisherman" who appears on the FBI Wanted-list in the episode following the "Trout Fishing in America Terrorists" chapter(41). Once again, Brautigan's vision reminds me of Thomas Pynchon, whose brilliant novel, *The Crying of Lot 49,* implies a latent alliance of all the cast-offs, drop-outs, and oddballs in American society, of all those suffering from "a hundred alienations."[11]

Indeed, it can be argued that instead of criticizing Brautigan for political irresponsibility—for constructing a bland "pastoral in the midst of death"—[12] one might see *Trout Fishing in America* (published five years ago but, according to Brautigan, written more like ten years ago) as a prophetic of the direction that protest would have to take in the United States. For, in his novel, Brautigan brings together frustrated students, anti-war activists and lawbreakers (it's significant that we don't even know what crime Richard Lawrence Marquette is supposed to have committed, as his wanted-poster has been trimmed along the edges), and he unites them loosely into a movement on the basis of their relationship to the true spirit of Trout Fishing in America. Ultimately, Brautigan is not writing a pastoral novel in *Trout Fishing in America.* Instead, he is writing an analysis of *why* the old pastoral myth of an America of freedom and

151

tranquility is no longer viable. . . . But to see this we must begin at the beginning and examine some of the early chapters of *Trout Fishing in America.*

As is usually the case with Brautigan's books, consideration of *Trout Fishing in America* begins not with the first chapter, but with the cover. Often Brautigan's covers are used to emphasize a main theme from one of the books. For instance, the cover of *Rommel Drives on Deep into Egypt* shows a smirking girl in a long military raincoat and high boots sitting in a sand-box, with an inverted pail and a shovel stuck in the sand in front of her; it serves as an ironic counterpoint to Rommel's futile military exploits, which, in terms of Brautigan's title poem, might also be described as playing in the sand. Similarly, the cover of *The Pill Versus the Springhill Mine Disaster* comments on the title poem of that volume by showing a slim, long-haired girl—emphatically not pregnant—seated tranquilly amid the rubble of something that resembles the entrance to a mine shaft. In *Trout Fishing in America,* though, Brautigan goes a step further. Not only does the anachronistic clothing of Brautigan and the girl with him on the cover emphasize the nostalgia for an older, simpler America that pervades his novel (and, by the fact that their outlandishly old-fashioned attire is once again fashionable among hippies, point up the relationship between today's counter culture and this lost America)—but also Brautigan frequently comments on his cover in the book itself.

The key to the cover of *Trout Fishing in America,* of course, is the statue of Benjamin Franklin in San Francisco's Washington Square. By evoking Franklin and locating him on the western edge of the North American continent, Brautigan brings together two of his central preoccupations—his concern with the American mythic or historical past and his more immediate concern with the West, with California. Benjamin Franklin has many roles in American history and legend: founding father, jack-of-all-trades, self-made man, homespun moralist and practical philosopher. He might be described, in Brautigan's terms, as a super, real-life Lee Mellon. In focusing on Franklin's optimism, Brautigan makes his opening cover-chapter an ironic keynote for the whole book. Kafka, Brautigan tells us, "learned about America by reading the autobiography of Benjamin Franklin . . . Kafka who said, 'I like the Americans because they are healthy and optimistic'"(2).

The irony of Franklin's role as a symbol of American optimism is enhanced by the fact that each of the four sides of the base of Franklin's statue bears the word "WELCOME." It might be said that this inscription adds the optimism of Horace Greeley's "Go West, young man," to Franklin's. (The statue itself, however, is rather forbidding; its "Welcome" is cold and stony.) Some of the other details in the opening chapter contribute to the establishment of an ironic mood of optimistic promise. Under a tall cypress tree behind the Franklin statue, Brautigan tells us, Adlai Stevenson had addressed a large crowd in his 1956 presidential campaign—Stevenson, who had so much faith in the optimistic notion that he could "talk sense to the American people"; Stevenson, so firmly rejected by the voters. Washington Square, we learn, is also a place where people eat the handouts they receive from the church across the street from the park, but sometimes the handouts are not quite what their recipients expect. "A friend of mine unwrapped his sandwich one afternoon and looked inside to find just a leaf of spinach. That was all"(2). Not even a flowerburger.

153

The second chapter, "Knock on Wood (Part One),"
continues the ironic theme of the promise of America.
It also includes the first reference to Trout Fishing in
America. The narrator thinks back to the first time he
heard of trout fishing in America, when he was a small
boy. His stepfather, he says, "had a way of describing
trout as if they were a precious and intelligent metal"
(3). Not as if they were silver—more like steel, something strong, firm, and cold. Thus, his first imaginative
response to trout had been somehow tied in with Pittsburgh and with Andrew Carnegie, another Benjamin
Franklin-style self-reliant hero. For Josephine Hendin, this
identification of trout and steel is a major example of
Brautigan's "psychic ache" that makes him long for an
emotionless cool.[13] But I think that Brautigan is rather
suggesting the strength and firmness—the power—of the
trout here, establishing in the mind of a small boy the
image of trout as a precious metal.

The chapter ends with an ironic "Reply of Trout Fishing in America"; he evokes what we might call the true
association of trout fishing in America—not steel mills
but "people with three cornered hats fishing in the
dawn"(3). This reference anticipates the later lyrical description of Lewis and Clark fishing below Great Falls
in 1805, in the dawn of America. Trout Fishing in America's reply suggests that the dream of trout fishing as
embodying the good life is anachronistic, an impossible
dream.

And, in the very next chapter, we see the boy of
"Knock on Wood (Part One)" trying for the first time
to realize his dream of trout fishing. This episode,
"Knock on Wood (Part Two)," reads like a burlesque
of a Norman Rockwell *Saturday Evening Post* cover or
like one of those dreadful "Just a-fishin' an' a-wishin'"

154

calendars that used to hang in everyone's kitchen. The narrator depicts himself as a poor (if not quite barefoot) boy without fishing tackle, who sees, as he thinks, a waterfall which he assumes must lead to a creek containing trout. "At last an opportunity to go trout fishing, to catch my first trout, to behold Pittsburgh"(4). He prepares "corny fishing tackle"—a bent pin, a piece of string, a slice of white bread for bait—and sets off for the waterfall, only to discover that "the waterfall was just a flight of white wooden stairs . . ."(5). He winds up as his own trout, eating the bread. The title of these two chapters has taken on another dimension; from "Knock on Wood" as an expression of hope, we have come to "Knock on Wood" as an expression of disappointment or frustration.

Once again, there is "The Reply of Trout Fishing in America," who, this time, says there was nothing he could do. "I couldn't change a flight of stairs into a creek"(5). Of course not, but, significantly, near the end of *Trout Fishing in America,* the narrator will learn that the Cleveland Wrecking Yard *can* perform the opposite miracle; he comes upon a stack of waterfalls, each one bearing a price-tag, in the used plumbing department of the Wrecking Yard. Already, within the first few pages, Brautigan has begun to develop two of his main themes: that there are sharply defined limits to the power of Trout Fishing in America ("There was nothing I could do"), and that it is not easy to get to the actual fishing.

In fact, in the next few episodes we might start to suspect that the narrator will never get to any real trout fishing at all. We might even feel that we're involved in a put-on or a shaggy dog story, that Brautigan's trout will prove elusive as Mark Twain's ram. Perhaps the

155

"Incidental intelligence" quoted on the back cover of the Delta edition of *Trout Fishing in America* will turn out to be true, that comment by a Viking Press editor: "Mr. Brautigan submitted a book to us in 1962 called TROUT FISHING IN AMERICA. I gather from the reports that it was not about trout fishing."

The next few episodes are like "Knock on Wood (Part Two)" in that they deal more with frustration than with the realization of the narrator's dream. In "Red Lip," the narrator has jumped seventeen years forward—to the near-past of the novel—and we see him trying unsuccessfully to hitch a ride downstream to Steelhead. This time he has real fishing equipment, but he can't reach the stream; he feels like an unwelcome intruder on the scene, an abandoned shack and its adjacent outhouse, "a monument . . . to a good ass gone under"(7). A few chapters later, we see the narrator near Grider Creek; now he even has a map "showing where the good fishing is"(14). But, once again, he has no car, no way of getting to the creek. Finally, in "Tom Martin Creek," he reaches his goal. "But that creek turned out to be a real son-of-a-bitch"(19). The fishing is bad, and he is plagued by such things as stubborn brush and poison oak. The actual experience of fishing is not what he'd imagined in his "Knock on Wood" hopeful childhood.

Which sends us back to one of the early chapters I've skipped over, "The Kool-Aid Wino." In itself, this episode is one of the most memorable as well as one of the funniest sections of *Trout Fishing in America*. We might wonder, however, what it has to do with the rest of the book. It is another childhood reminiscence, an account of a friend of the narrator who, absurdly enough, "became a Kool-Aid wino as the result of a rupture"(8).

The narrator describes the elaborate, even ritualistic motions his friend went through every day to obtain and prepare his daily fix, his much-diluted, unsugared gallon of grape Kool-Aid. "To him the making of Kool-Aid was a romance and ceremony"(9). The boy's life centered around his Kool-Aid ritual so much that his perceptions were altered by his obsession. The chapter ends, "He created his own Kool-Aid reality and was able to illuminate himself by it"(10).

Taken by itself, "The Kool-Aid Wino" would seem to suggest the power of imagination (whether symbolized by Kool-Aid, watermelontrout oil, or a candlelion) to transcend the dull, humdrum limits of reality. The boy in the story is able to get around his disabling rupture and his family's poverty as easily as he ignores his mother's request that he do the dishes. However, "The Kool-Aid Wino" has to be seen in relation to other episodes in *Trout Fishing in America*. Specifically, it has to be looked at as a contrast to "Knock on Wood (Part Two)," in which, as I've said, the narrator perceives a staircase as a waterfall, only to be disappointed when he arrives to fish beneath his imagined waterfall. Except in the most limited and controlled imaginative visions, reality is likely to intrude, to disappoint and frustrate.

The emphasis on "ceremony" in "The Kool-Aid Wino" suggests a connection with another early chapter in *Trout Fishing in America*—the puzzling "Another Method of Making Walnut Catsup." As I've said in my discussion of *In Watermelon Sugar*, Brautigan evidently considers custom, ceremony, and ritual as important devices for controlling one's life. The ceremonial aspect of "The Kool-Aid Wino" is paralleled by the highly ritualized cookbook language which Brautigan mimics in "Walnut Catsup." The cookbook makes an ideal symbol for the controlled, coherent life; in a recipe, everything works out smoothly. The narrator imagines Trout Fishing in America (here embodied as "a rich gourmet"[11]) and Maria Callas, his girlfriend (I assume that any famous and glamorous American woman would have served as well), sitting down to a wildly miscellaneous succession of dishes. For each dish, we are given a detailed recipe. As in "The Kool-Aid Wino" chapter, the implication is that as long as one follows the "romance and . . . ceremony" of the formula, all will be well. The moon comes out, Maria Callas sings, "And Trout Fishing in America and Maria Callas poured walnut catsup on their hamburgers"(12).

In imaginative fantasy, the narrator is able to perceive a controlled, coherent, ceremonial situation in which things work out smoothly. The closest real equivalent to the banquet in "Another Method of Making Walnut Catsup" is the relationship between the ex-convict and ex-whore in "Room 208, Hotel Trout Fishing in America." The "good world" these two people have constructed for themselves consists of a shabby hotel room containing some plants and a single burner hot plate, on which the woman "could really cook up a good meal, fancy dishes, too . . ."(69). But their good world is not invulnerable. The pimp who had forced the woman to hustle for him has run up numerous bills that they're still paying off, and he remains in the background as a physical threat, having broken into their room many times to menace them. As a result, the room is like a fortress; on the door there are "about a hundred locks, bolts and chains and anchors and steel spikes and canes filled with acid"(68). In addition, the ex-medical student ex-con has a loaded gun always ready to fend off the angry pimp. Significantly, the gun sits—in this room in which "everything was in its proper place"(68)—right next to a bowl of goldfish.

This juxtaposition of gun and goldfish—latent violence and gentle tranquility, external danger and internal calm—is important in the overall thematic development of *Trout Fishing in America*. Actual or latent violence is in fact one of the dominant motifs in the book. Brautigan's vision of America is heavily colored by his awareness of impending violence. Almost surely, he would agree with Rap Brown that violence is as American as cherry pie, though he might prefer to say as American as walnut catsup.

The early episode, "Prologue to Grider Creek," which seems to have nothing at all to do with the following "Grider Creek" chapter, first throws out this important theme of violence. Indeed, it might better be called "Prologue to Violence." Unlike most of the episodes in *Trout Fishing in America*, "Prologue to Grider Creek" is set in Middle America, in Mooresville, Indiana, "the John Dillinger capital of America"(13). Here, in Dillinger's hometown, Brautigan sets an unpleasant little tale about a man who is bothered by rats in his basement. He obtains a .38 revolver, goes down to the cellar, and systematically begins shooting rats. The rats remain unperturbed, with those which haven't yet been shot feeding on the bodies of those which have. "They acted as if it were a movie and started eating their dead companions for popcorn"(13).

The setting is perfect. The man functions as an agent of civilization (or law and order), efficiently wiping out the alien vermin; in the John Dillinger capital, the rats play Dillinger to the man's J. Edgar Hoover. Only, there's something chilling, unnatural, inhuman about the man's extermination of the "child-eyed" rats. We get the feeling that the man enjoys his work too much. We might think of this episode much later in *Trout Fishing in America* when we read the narrator's recollection of how he declined to kill the gartersnakes he "deported" from the garden of the old lady he worked for as a child(82). More important, in "The Salt Creek Coyotes," Brautigan writes about the practice of exterminating coyotes by leaving out cyanide capsules.[14] Here, he makes an explicit comparison between the wanton killing of animal pests and the practice of capital punishment. The overall effect is to create an image of a society that can only get rid of its nuisances by violent means—the destruction of rats and coyotes or of Dillinger and Caryl Chessman.

In general, Brautigan is sympathetic toward such American outlaws and pariahs as Dillinger, Billy the Kid, Pretty Boy Floyd, Caryl Chessman. This sympathy can be seen as an extension of the feeling throughout Brautigan's work for losers, underdogs, outcasts of all kinds. It's no coincidence that Jesse and Lee Mellon see themselves as old-fashioned Western badmen when they shake down the two frightened boys in *A Confederate General from Big Sur;* they *are* outlaws in so far as they try to exist outside the boundaries of American society, just as the "Trout Fishing in America Terrorists" are terrorists in so far as they threaten the conventional educational structure by their whimsical exploits.

Similarly, the narrator, his woman, and their infant daughter are in effect depicted as outlaws as they move around looking for a "good world" of their own. The America presented in *Trout Fishing in America* is an angry, crowded, violent place. In "The Teddy Roosevelt Chingader," the narrator and his small family are first treated to a lecture on the Communist menace by a

160

Mormon girl, then greeted by a very threatening no-fishing sign (" IF YOU FISH IN THIS CREEK, WE'LL HIT YOU IN THE HEAD"[60]), and finally the narrator is denounced bitterly by a clerk in a store where he stops to buy a candy bar: "You're better off dead, you Commie bastard"(60). When at last they reach their objective, Big Redfish Lake, the campgrounds are as crowded as a sordid skidrow hotel; they move on to a virtually abandoned campground at Little Redfish Lake, where the narrator is surprised to find that the stovepipe on the camp stove they use is *not* riddled with bullets. His expression of surprise at this negative fact makes a perfect climax to this chapter mingling the pastoral impulse and the potentially violent mood pervading this angry land. "Almost all the camp stoves we had seen in Idaho had been full of bullet holes. I guess it's only reasonable that people, when they get the chance, would want to shoot some old stove sitting in the woods"(62). (Especially, one might add, if there are no rats or coyotes or other living things available for shooting.)

The very end of the "Teddy Roosevelt Chingader" episode brings us indirectly back to the opening chapter, with its focus on Benjamin Franklin. The narrator describes a wooden table with benches fastened to it, which he says reminds him of a pair of old-fashioned Benjamin Franklin glasses, "the ones with those funny square lenses." He sits down on one of the benches ("the left lens") and looks out at the Sawtooth Mountains. "Like astigmatism," he concludes the chapter, "I made myself at home"(62). He squints out toward the gentle pastoral America—toward the illusion he has been pursuing since his childhood.

The narrator, of course, is not alone in his quest for

an illusionary America. In another Little Redfish Lake episode, "The Surgeon," he meets a doctor who is moving restlessly around the West looking for *his* good world. The doctor is a contrast to the narrator in just about every respect except for their mutual love of fishing and their restlessness. He is a solid, rock-ribbed conservative, who tells the narrator he wouldn't practice medicine if it became "socialized" in the United States, and who is appalled by a tax structure that pays a man for not working: "I'll get twelve hundred dollars back in income tax returns by not working any more this year. . . . I don't understand this country"(72). He seeks an America characterized by his conception of freedom—what Charles Reich would call a Consciousness I America—where he can practice medicine any way he wants and where he'll have plenty of time for fishing and hunting. The narrator's conception of the doctor's quest is of course equally appropriate to the narrator himself: ". . . he was leaving for America, often only a place in the mind"(72).

The America that both the narrator and the doctor seek is essentially the one evoked by Trout Fishing in America near the very beginning of the book: "people with three-cornered hats fishing in the dawn." The contrast between this mythic America—this place in the mind—and the real America is made even clearer in the powerful "The Last Time I Saw Trout Fishing in America" episode. In this climactic chapter, the narrator and Trout Fishing in America meet shortly after the death of Hemingway (another of those who sought the mythic America) and discuss Great Falls, Montana, where the narrator had lived for awhile as a child. The narrator's memories of "the twelve least important things ever said about Great Falls, Montana"(91), including a dim recollection of an old Deanna Durbin movie that has somehow gotten mixed up with his memory of the Missouri River. For the narrator (as, surely, for today's tourist), Great Falls is the boring nowhere American town, a Montana equivalent of the Texas town in Larry McMurtry's *The Last Picture Show*. Trout Fishing in America, however, remembers the day Lewis and Clark discovered Great Falls and fished for trout below the falls. "That was June 13, 1805"(91), long ago in a lost America.

But the myth dies hard. In "A Note on the Camping Craze That Is Currently Sweeping America," the narrator spins off a sad and very funny imaginative fantasy which burlesques the idea of nature—fishing and camping—as curative. This episode concerns a man named Norris and begins with him sitting in a San Francisco bar, "having a few." He gets talking to another man, and in their dialogue we learn that Mr. Norris has pretty much botched up his life. "I've had three wives and I can't remember the names of my children"(73). Mr. Norris is somewhat like Mr. Henly, in "The Wild Birds of Heaven," and Roy Earle, in *A Confederate General from Big Sur*—an outwardly successful man living on the edge of desperation. His barroom acquaintance recommends that he "go out camping, try a little trout fishing. Trout fishing is one of the best things in the world for remembering children's names"(73).

The next morning, Mr. Norris goes to a sporting goods store and charges vast quantities of camping and fishing equipment. Then he sets out to loaf and invite his soul. Unfortunately, he finds that the first sixteen camping grounds he tries are all jammed with campers. Luckily for him, in the seventeenth a man has just died of a heart attack, so Mr. Norris is able to take over his spot and set up his camp there. However, during the night, some men bring a corpse (presumably that of the person who'd died earlier) to Mr. Norris' campsite and leave it propped against his tent. He wakes up in time to catch the "body bringers" and he makes them take the corpse away with them. A few minutes later, he hears another camper also refusing to harbor the corpse.

This strange tale emphasizes several of the themes of *Trout Fishing in America*—the frenzied rush for the therapeutic life in nature, the absurdity of bringing one's affluence along with one (Mr. Norris has practically a whole sporting goods store with him), and the uncomfortable presence of the dead among the living campers. Mr. Norris—like the surgeon and like the narrator himself—is one of those who has gone to "look for America" (to borrow Paul Simon's phrase), but he has found a kind of graveyard instead.

Mr. Norris' strange encounter with the body bringers occurs two-thirds of the way into *Trout Fishing in America*, but death has been a frequent presence throughout Brautigan's novel. In one of the early fishing episodes, "Trout Fishing on the Bevel," the action is set at Graveyard Creek, which gets its name from the fact that it runs between two graveyards. One graveyard seems to be reserved for the corpses of affluent people; it is well kept, with "fine marble headstones and statues and tombs." The other is for the poor: "There were no fancy headstones for the poor dead. Their markers were small boards that looked like heels of stale bread"(20). The fishing is good at Graveyard Creek, but the narrator is bothered by "the poverty of the dead"(21). Their ill-kept graves—marked by faded wooden boards and decorated with wilted flowers left by their equally impoverished survivors—start the narrator imagining the grim lives that must have preceded these shabby deaths:

"Devoted Slob Father Of . . . Beloved Worked-to-Death Mother Of . . ."(20). Death and violence are never far apart, of course; one of the graves commemorates an eighteen-year-old who "Had His Ass Shot Off/In a Honky-Tonk"(21). The narrator concludes this moving episode by telling us that he once had a vision of himself gathering up all the dead grass, old fruit jars and tin cans, wooden markers, wilted flowers—all the poverty-stricken artifacts of this dismal graveyard—"and tying a fly with all that stuff and then going outside and casting it up into the sky, watching it float over clouds and then into the evening star"(21). Through an act of imagination, he would (if he could) gather up and banish the painful indignity of "the poverty of the dead."

But the presence of death is not that easy to exorcise from the world of *Trout Fishing in America*. In fact, the next several episodes in the novel, following "Trout Fishing on the Bevel," are all concerned directly or indirectly with death. The very next chapter, "Sea Sea Rider," is explicitly linked by the narrator's description of the bookstore in which the action takes place as "a parking lot for used graveyards"(22). More important, the owner of the bookstore is one of death's rejects; he has survived a heart attack and being torpedoed in the North Atlantic. He presides over his repository of grave-yards as one whom "death did not want"(22).

The episode is set in what the narrator calls "that terrible year of 1959," in other words, about a year before the time of the main trout fishing chapters in *Trout Fishing in America*, about a year before the narrator's quest for his good world. The narrator depicts himself as a strangely melancholy figure during this terrible year, rather like Jesse, in *A Confederate General from Big Sur*, who has to make a conscious effort to pretend to

165

be human. He is reading a book about Billy the Kid—
that half-legendary figure so in love with death and
violence—who was born, as the narrator troubles to tell
us, in 1859—just one hundred years before "that terrible
year of 1959." A curious coincidence—or maybe more
than that.

As the narrator goes on to relate his strange experience with a rich man and his beautiful girlfriend, the
number 59 comes up twice more. The owner of the
bookstore abruptly asks the narrator if he wants to get
laid. Although he declines—preoccupied as he is with the
short violent life of Billy the Kid—before he really knows
what's happening, the narrator finds himself upstairs having sexual intercourse with the girl (the sex act is described as "the eternal 59th second when it becomes a
minute"[24]), while the man (who, according to the
girl, is fabulously rich, the owner of 3,859 Rolls Royces)
looks on, fully dressed and seemingly without emotion.

After this oddly joyless sexual encounter, the woman
dresses and leaves with the man, both of them calmly
discussing where they'll have dinner. The bookstore
owner, that quirky Pandarus, reappears to "explain" to the
narrator "what happened up there" (24). His bizarre
explanation consists of two different little stories: one
deals with an ultimately unsuccessful love affair between
a young Communist and a woman painter, ending in
their separation; the other "explanation" reads like a
pornographic spurious episode from the career of Billy
the Kid, about the prolonged sexual revels of a teen-aged
gunslinger and an even younger Mexican girl. The ending of this little tale almost makes the connection with
Billy the Kid explicit: "Neither of you lived to be
twenty-one. It was not necessary"(26).

Understandably, the narrator does not feel illuminated

166

by the bookstore owner's version of what happened upstairs. The owner sees the narrator's sexual encounter in the terms of either sentimental romance or lurid pornography. He sees the encounter through his imagination (through what we might call, by analogy to "The Kool-Aid Wino," his "bookstore reality"). But to the narrator, as to the woman and her escort, nothing much happened up there. The sexual act is depicted as virtually meaningless in this episode. It is still the terrible year of 1959; nothing has changed. The woman and the man go off to dinner. The narrator remains surrounded by graveyards; he returns to his book about the doomed Billy the Kid.

The death motif continues in the next chapter, "The Last Year the Trout Came up Hayman Creek." Hayman Creek, we learn, was named after a man named Charles Hayman, who settled there in 1876. Again, the date is important (as dates—and numbers in general—usually are in Brautigan). For this episode is not only a kind of elegy for Hayman—"Gone now the old fart" (27)—but also, in a sense, for the pioneer spirit and for the frontier itself.

1876 was of course the one-hundredth birthday of the United States. As we know from the writings of people like Whitman, Mark Twain, and Henry Adams, this American centennial was loaded with bitterly ironic overtones, coming at a time when the country was sunk in political corruption and at the mercy of ruthless financial manipulators—when much of the early promise and idealism of America seemed long gone. Indeed, as undoubtedly many writers will be pointing out in the next four years, the widespread disillusionment in the United States at its hundredth birthday was similar in many respects to what we may assume the mood of a

167

large part of the nation will be at its *two*-hundreth celebration. In addition, although the official closing of the frontier was still some years off, by 1876 there wasn't very much good free land left in America, millions of acres having been swallowed up by the railroad giants.

Thus, it's quite appropriate that Brautigan should elegize Charles Hayman in *Trout Fishing in America*. Hayman is presented as a mean-spirited ascetic, who never "had a cup of coffee, a smoke, a drink or a woman and thought he'd be a fool if he did"(27). He was a "half-assed pioneer," who settled on land which Brautigan describes as "poor and ugly and horrible"(27). Hayman could almost be called a travesty of the Pioneer Spirit (or even, perhaps, of the Spirit of '76)—an unfriendly, ungenerous hermit scratching out a very primitive living. And yet not quite a travesty, for Hayman is given two qualities that Brautigan obviously admires— independence (he raises his own food, grinds his own wheat, is completely self-sufficient) and, in his misanthrope way, a reverence for Nature. This latter quality is emphasized by Brautigan's telling us that after Hayman died the trout never came up Hayman Creek again, and when "planted" there by fish and game workers years later, the trout immediately died.

This quality of reverence for Nature (or life, finally) takes us directly into the next episode, "Trout Death by Port Wine." At first reading, this chapter might seem to be nothing more than an amusing mock-elegy for an eleven-inch rainbow trout that died from a drink of port wine. The sketch is, in fact, somewhat reminiscent of that humorous idyllic interlude in Hemingway's *The Sun Also Rises*, in which Jake Barnes and Bill Gorton get drunk while fishing (for trout, needless to say) in the mountains of Spain. Here, though, only the narrator

168

does the fishing, while his friend restricts himself to kibitzing and drinking. When the narrator catches his first trout, his friend pours a slug of port into its mouth and the trout spasms and dies.

This occasions a long catalogue of trout fishing erudition on the narrator's part. He lists a couple of dozen books dealing with trout fishing, in none of which is there any reference to a trout o.d.-ing on port wine. Despite the burlesque implications of the narrator's trout bibliography and despite the general levity of the episode (the friend is given to wild flights of fancy, in which, for example, a trout fly reminds him of "Evangeline's vagina"[31]), I believe that Brautigan is essentially serious in this chapter and that he wants us to be put off by the friend's high jinks. In contrast to Mr. Hayman of the preceding chapter, the narrator's friend is not a person who has reverence for life or Nature.

I believe that Brautigan means it when he says that "It is against the natural order of death for a trout to die by having a drink of port wine"(29). Once again, Brautigan shows kinship to Hemingway. As Hemingway's Old Man, Santiago, celebrated the death of the giant marlin he killed in equal struggle but mourned the destruction of the fish's body by sharks later, so the narrator of *Trout Fishing in America* seems to feel that a "natural" death is in the natural order of things: whether from accident (disease or draught), from predators (birds or humans), or even from ecological imbalance (a river polluted from excessive human excrement—though presumably *not* from industrial waste).

Killing the trout as a careless joke is "another thing" (29); it is something degrading as well as unnatural. Surely Brautigan means us to relate the poisoning of the trout with port to the poisoning of coyotes with cyanide, in "The Salt Creek Coyotes." In that sketch, as I've said, the narrator's train of thought leads him to connect the coyotes and such victims of capital punishment as Caryl Chessman. Here, he does the same sort of thing in a different way, by describing the trout in its death spasm as if it were human: "The mouth was wide open and chattering almost as if it had human teeth"(32).

The narrator's friend is finally an intruder, a despoiler of Paradise. And Owl Snuff Creek, the setting for "Trout Death by Port Wine," is presented as a kind of paradise, as a good place the narrator has been seeking all his life. Significantly, in this episode the narrator makes an indirect allusion to his frustrated initial attempt at trout fishing, as a child. On that occasion, as I've said, the "waterfall" that led to his promised trout stream turned out to be a wooden staircase. But now the narrator refers to a real waterfall in a canyon as if it were a staircase: "I fished downstream coming ever closer and closer to the narrow staircase of the canyon"(31). For a moment, the narrator has almost realized his childhood vision, but the vision is marred by the buffoonery of his friend.

Brautiganian logic being what it is—a thing of rapid transitions and apparent *non sequiturs*—it's only a short step from a fine rainbow trout killed by port wine to a fantasy in which the narrator imagines the mythic figure of Trout Fishing in America as a corpse preserved in a large cask of whiskey: "The Autopsy of Trout Fishing in America." The details of the imagined death and autopsy, however, are taken from (of all things!) the biography of Lord Byron, rather than from any American experience, real or imagined. A strange fancy—to present

170

the autopsy of Trout Fishing in America "as if Trout Fishing in America had been Lord Byron and had died in Missolonghi, Greece..."(33)—but I think this very brief episode works in well with the preceding chapter.

By identifying Trout Fishing in America with Byron, Brautigan emphasizes this mythic figure's role as a spirit of rebellion and freedom. Byron, of course, had gone to Greece to fight for Greek independence. Byron is also a famous example of the banished exile, as is Trout Fishing in America in this episode: "O, a long way from Idaho..."(33). Finally, I think that by depicting Trout Fishing in America as dead, Brautigan is commenting indirectly on "Trout Death by Port Wine," that he is saying, in effect, that the narrator's friend has banished and murdered the true spirit of Trout Fishing in America through his lack of reverence for Nature. Virtually throughout the novel, Trout Fishing in America takes the form of (or informs the spirit of) persons or movements that represent a reverence for life, even though as the book goes on the positive figures identified with Trout Fishing in America become increasingly exiled, outlawed, strange. One way of describing the late chapter, "The Last Time I Saw Trout Fishing in America," would be to say that this final meeting represents the narrator's acceptance of the banishment of the spirit of Trout Fishing in America; that spirit may have flourished in the American dawn of Lewis and Clark, but not in the America of the 1960s.

At one point in the novel, Brautigan appears to identify Trout Fishing in America with the singularly inappropriate figure of Jack the Ripper; this compulsive psychopathic killer wears "a costume of trout fishing in America" (48). He is, we are told, "The Mayor of the Twentieth Century." Surely no one could have less of the kind of reverence for life I've been talking about. The important point about Jack the Ripper's costume, of course, is that it *is* a costume, that is to say, a disguise. And, as Brautigan says, "The disguise was perfect"(48). The figure of Jack the Ripper is an appropriate metaphor for the latent senseless violence and death pervading *Trout Fishing in America;* in disguising himself as Trout Fishing in America (as his real opposite, we might say), Jack the Ripper has replaced the gentle figure of Trout Fishing in America, has, once again, banished him.

The "legless, screaming middle-aged wino"(45), Trout Fishing in America Shorty, who appears three separate times in the novel, is another example of the perversion of the Trout Fishing in America image. This "evil fart," consciously borrowed from Nelson Algren's Railroad Shorty, is quite literally a chopped-off version of Trout Fishing in America. The narrator and his friend plan to get rid of him, to ship him off to Algren in Chicago, but instead this degenerate equivalent of the spirit of freedom and independence disappears. In a striking brief burlesque of the Open Road motif—so important in American literature from Whitman to Kerouac—the narrator imagines Trout Fishing in America Shorty pedalling "down to San Jose in his wheelchair, rattling along the freeway at a quarter of a mile an hour"(47).

Later, he reappears in San Francisco, like a bad penny, and we learn that he has become a cult figure: "The movies have discovered him"(63). Here, the narrator is satirizing the tendency of our society to make a hero, a personality, out of virtually anyone. For who could be less promising material for such a role? Speculating on the use the movies might make of Trout Fishing in America Shorty's career (if that's the word), the narrator says, "They'll milk it for all it's worth and make cream and butter from a pair of empty pants legs and a low budget"(63). In a commercialized America, Leonardo da Vinci would be commissioned to turn out trout fishing lures; so, out of the unpromising material of Trout Fishing in America Shorty, the society makes what it can—a phony "New Wave" movie hero.

"The Last Mention of Trout Fishing in America Shorty" puts things back in perspective. The narrator begins with a mock-heroic build-up concerning the circumstances under which his daughter was conceived. At that time, he says, he "had no idea the child . . . would ever meet Trout Fishing in America Shorty"(96). When the baby does encounter this legless grotesque as he sits in his wheelchair in the shadow of the Benjamin Franklin statue (that statue from Chapter One which casts its shadow over the whole novel), Trout Fishing in America Shorty tries to charm her. But she very sensibly chooses to play in a sandbox instead of sitting in his lap. Perhaps Brautigan means this chapter to be a contrast to the preceding Trout Fishing in America shorty episode. The baby's innocence is wisdom compared to the absurd adulation that is given to Trout Fishing in America Shorty in his career as a movie star.

In terms of *Trout Fishing in America* as a whole, we can say that both Jack the Ripper and Trout Fishing in America Shorty are important as distortions or perversions of the true spirit of Trout Fishing in America. Jack the Ripper disguises himself as the gentle spirit of life and freedom to commit sudden, violent murders. Trout Fishing in America Shorty is the debased, urbanized, and finally commercialized modern equivalent of the spirit of the open road. Taken together, they emphasize Brautigan's point that it has become more

173

and more difficult—maybe ultimately impossible—to meet or discover the true Trout Fishing in America.

Even in those episodes that do seem genuinely pastoral, that do seem to be presided over by the true spirit of Trout Fishing in America, an alien presence may be at least hinted at. Why else, in the wonderful "Hunchback Trout" chapter, would Brautigan mention that the cutthroat trout "fly the orange banner of Jack the Ripper"(55)? Why else his insistence that a friendly young shepherd "looked like a young, skinny Adolf Hitler"(34), another "Mayor of the Twentieth Century," so to speak?

The latency of violence and death pervading *Trout Fishing in America*[15] is never very far from the narrator's mind. Although there is development in the narrator as a character—from the listless, apathetic young man in "Sea Sea Rider" to the far more involved, active, energetic person later on—he is never quite free from anxiety or the shadow of depression. None of the protagonists in Brautigan's novels are. We should not be surprised when the narrator of *Trout Fishing in America* reports favorably the plan two of his friends have to spend the winter in an insane asylum. He says, "No winter spent there could be a total loss"(18). Like the library in *The Abortion,* an insane asylum can be seen as a refuge from "the fickle wind of the Twentieth Century"(92). The narrator's attempted refuge, on the other hand, is his search for a "good world" in the wandering province of Trout Fishing in America.

But, as I've suggested, the very things he's fleeing are either already present or imminent. In this regard, "Worsewick" is one of the central chapters in *Trout Fishing in America.* This episode (more than one-third of the way into the novel) contains the first explicit

174

reference to the narrator's woman and their baby. Looked at in bare outline, the chapter seems to be one of the genuine pastoral moments in the novel—and there aren't too many of those. The little family of wanderers pause to bathe at Worsewick Hot Springs. After a while, the narrator becomes sexually aroused (almost the only time he does in the whole book), and after he puts the baby out of the way, in the car, he and his woman make love in the warm water. If we look at the details that Brautigan fills this episode with, however, we get a rather different feeling about "Worsewick." First of all, the hot springs are more like a graveyard than like a curative bath. As they dabble in the water, the narrator and his family are surrounded by "dozens of dead fish" which had "made the mistake of going down the creek too far..."(43). Second, the love-making is governed by the anxiety of the narrator and his woman, who, quite literally, fear to bring children into the world. The narrator says, "I didn't want any more kids for a long time"(44). Consequently, the narrator withdraws before ejaculation, sending his sperm into the warm, scummy water. The final details of the chapter bring together the two major motifs—the reluctance to create new life and the prevalence of death: "...I saw a dead fish come forward and float into my sperm, bending it in the middle. His eyes were stiff like iron"(44).

Practically the only central chapter in *Trout Fishing in America* that doesn't contain ominous or unpleasant overtones is "The Pudding Master of Stanley Basin," which deals with an afternoon spent catching minnows in a pan containing the remnants of a vanilla pudding. That the episode deals with minnows rather than trout seems to me to be of some significance. The interlude is a pleasant and mildly amusing (especially in terms

175

of the contrast between the "scientific" engineering student who contrives an elaborate device for catching minnows and suffers "two hours of intimate and universal failure"(64), and the woman who catches a panful of minnows by sheer chance), but, after all, the activity is chiefly for the entertainment of the narrator's baby daughter, who plays with the minnows for an hour or so before growing bored.

We are far from the shining vision of the narrator in the early "Knock on Wood" chapters. Indeed, for its apparent looseness of structure, *Trout Fishing in America* moves fairly steadily, even inevitably, toward the narrator's final farewell to Trout Fishing in America. The America the narrator has been able to discover is just too far removed from the place Lewis and Clark come upon with wonder in 1805. There is no good world to be won in following Trout Fishing in America.

Briefly—and I think anticlimactically—the narrator tries another version of the pastoral, settling with his family and two friends in a small cabin in Mill Valley, California. The terms of their escape, this time, are more or less similar to the "secession" in *A Confederate General from Big Sur*. But this is not the America of 1876—of Charles Hayman settling on the little creek that later bore his name—either; we are much closer to 1976, and the days of homesteading in the wilderness are long gone. The cabin in the California bush is not even theirs; they are merely renting it for the summer. Already, in the second of the two brief chapters devoted to this interlude, "Footnote Chapter to 'Red Lip,'" the narrator refers to this experience as a thing of the past.

Finally, the nostalgic dream of a simple life of freedom and self-reliance winds up, like that trout stream from Colorado, in the Cleveland Wrecking Yard. The

Wrecking Yard, of course, is Brautigan's major symbol for the commercializing tendencies of our society. It is a place where even Nature itself can be transported, cut up into lengths, measured accurately, stacked neatly, inventoried, and put up for sale.

Trout Fishing in America concludes with "The Mayonnaise Chapter," which, even more than the early "Another Method of Making Walnut Catsup," seems to have no relation to the rest of the book. In part, I suppose we could say that by ending his novel with a *non sequitur* Brautigan is indicating that we shouldn't spoil our birthdays trying to work out the structure of the book. As I've said in discussing his poems, there's frequently a tendency in Brautigan to forestall criticism by disparaging his own work (the "so what?" quality I mentioned in "Haiku Ambulance"). But one thing that I think we should note in "The Mayonnaise Chapter" is the reference to "the passing of Mr. Good"(112). "Mr. Good" may be considered as one final name for the spirit of Trout Fishing in America, pursued throughout the book, elegized in the book. In this sense, the entire novel—from the wooden staircase of Portland to the Cleveland Wrecking Yard—has led to the narrator's final reluctant acceptance of "the passing of Mr. Good."

Looking back over this long chapter, I realize that I have belabored some of the relationships and structural aspects of *Trout Fishing in America* pretty badly. In fact, I suppose I have done both of the things I said I'd try not to do: I have wrenched the book to make things fit; I have passed over certain details and even a few episodes. On the first count, I must repeat a point that I've tried to make in just about every chapter in this book, in one form or another. The general tendency

177

among Brautigan's critics is to regard his books as form-less and ultimately trivial; at times, especially in his poems, Brautigan seems to lend support to this view. So, if I've made *Trout Fishing in America* seem schematic or mechanical (and I'm sure I have, in places), I hope I have also shown that there is control, organization—*art*—present in the novel. On the second count, I have discussed the vast majority of the episodes in *Trout Fishing in America* in this chapter, and I have pursued a couple of side issues in footnotes. I think that most, if not quite all, of the material that I have skipped over could have been worked into my discussion, but to do this would be to go on at intolerably tedious length.

In my opinion, a more damaging criticism to be raised concerning my approach to *Trout Fishing in America* is that in taking Brautigan's novel so seriously I have neglected Brautigan's humor and zaniness. As I said in discussing *A Confederate General from Big Sur*, to write a funny book is in itself a considerable achievement, and except for *Confederate General*, *Trout Fishing in America* is surely Brautigan's funniest novel. In general, throughout his work, Brautigan's best humorous effects come from exaggeration or distortion, from what Jesse refers to in *Confederate General* as "a wonderful sense of distortion"(82). As in nineteenth-century American Tall Tale humor, Brautigan often balances his sense of distortion against mundane circumstantial details so that we accept—for a moment too long—the fantastic implications of what we're being told. Thus, to use the best example in *Trout Fishing in America*, Brautigan prefaces his first reference to the used trout stream for sale in the Cleveland Wrecking Yard by a page-and-a-half description of the ruins of an old mansion near Big Sur. The first mention of the trout stream is very casual and matter-of-fact: "My own experience with the Cleveland Wrecking Yard began two days ago when I heard about a used trout stream they had on sale out at the Yard"(103). Then he drops the subject for another half-page, as if it requires no comment, to describe an overheard conversation between two young black boys who are passionately interested in Chubby Checker and the Twist. When he circles back to the Cleveland Wrecking Yard and the used trout stream, he continues to treat his incredible subject in a deadpan tone, as if it were no more unusual than a ruined mansion, Chubby Checker, or the idea of making a Wrecking Yard "THE FAMILY GIFT CENTER"(104). Similarly, in "The Hunchback Trout," Brautigan mingles the fantasy of fishing as telephone repairing with concise, authentic descriptive detail concerning the actual fishing.

Throughout *Trout Fishing in America*, there are, of course, examples of incongruous juxtapositions (what I've previously called Brautiganian logic). Indeed, it could be said, as I've suggested earlier, that the entire structure of *Trout Fishing in America* is based on connections between apparently unconnected details or ideas—the Kool-Aid ritual leads directly to the ceremonies of "Another Method of Making Walnut Catsup," the impoverished graveyard of "Trout Fishing on the Bevel" to the used graveyard of books in "Sea Sea Rider," the alcohol death of a trout to the alcohol embalming of Trout Fishing in America, and so forth. Also, throughout the novel, there are examples of Brautigan's good eye for incongruous details and ear for absurd dialogue—Trout Fishing in America Shorty taking to the Open Road at a quarter-mile an hour, a dog so old it had become a stuffed dog, a savage

179

cat that believes it is the last cat in the world; the drunken dialogue between Mr. Norris and his barroom companion (in "A Note on the Camping Craze That Is Currently Sweeping America"), the conversation at loggerheads between a gas station attendant who wants to give away wild flower seeds and a man who just wants to buy gasoline (in "Trout Fishing on the Street of Eternity"). Even more than in his other books, in *Trout Fishing in America* Brautigan continually displays his ability to perceive the bizarre in the ordinary.

In quantity—if a thing like humor could be measured quantitatively—*Trout Fishing in America* might contain even more humor than *Confederate General*. In a few places, however, I find Brautigan a little heavy-handed in *Trout Fishing in America*—for example, in the belabored account of "Witness for Trout Fishing in America Peace," where he presents a sarcastic view of a peace demonstration as seen by a paranoid anti-Communist. On the whole, though, when Brautigan tries for humorous effects in *Trout Fishing in America,* he is very funny, indeed, sometimes hilarious. I have stressed the serious and even grim implications of *Trout Fishing in America* because these seem to me less apparent than the book's humorous qualities. In my view, *Trout Fishing in America* is at least as sad as it is funny; certainly it is far more pessimistic about life in these United States in the second half of the twentieth century than it is optimistic.

For all of my talk about the overall structure of *Trout Fishing in America,* I suppose that many (or even most) readers will remember the book by its parts—the strange account of "The Kool-Aid Wino," the misadventures of "The Trout Fishing in America Terrorists," the indoor pastoral in "Room 208, Hotel Trout Fishing in America," the outdoor pastoral in "The Hunchback Trout," the brilliant burlesque of progress and efficiency in "The Cleveland Wrecking Yard"—there are so many memorable episodes and details. *Trout Fishing in America* is the shortest of Brautigan's four novels, but it seems to *contain* the most. Robert Adams rates *Trout Fishing in America* below *In Watermelon Sugar* because of his personal "preference for more controlled books. . . ."[16] But, as Adams acknowledges, one could argue from the opposite direction and prefer *Trout Fishing in America* for its crowded multiplicity of episodes, for its sprawl— for its bounty. In my view, the real triumph of *Trout Fishing in America* is its combination of bounty and control. It is a hard book to discuss coherently, and it must have been a difficult book to put together. It would have to be, for it is ultimately a very ambitious book. Finally, *Trout Fishing in America*—in its combination of satire and nostalgia, of elegy and humor, of realistic description and fantasy—lives up to Brautigan's statement about it in *Revenge of the Lawn,* where he refers to the book as notes "toward a vision of America"(37).

Conclusion.
Brautigan in the American Grain

At one point in *A Confederate General from Big Sur*, Jesse tells us that he had been reading a book on the soul. He goes on to say, "I approached it as a mystery novel"(66). Some of Brautigan's admirers would likewise prefer to approach his books as mystery novels, exempt from critical analysis or judgments. I quote from a recent letter to the Editor of the *New York Times Book Review:* "There's just one way to approach Brautigan, and that's to float along with his prose. Don't waste your time trying to be *involved*—with what he does or doesn't do."[1] The writer of this letter claims, further on, that "Richard" (as he calls him) would agree with his advice to "would-be analysts."

And, indeed, Richard probably would agree. As I've said in several places in this study, Brautigan is pretty consistently anti-literary throughout his books. At times, his attitude toward his own work seems defensive (the "so what?" tendency); at other times, he is amused and mocking about criticism in general, as in "Critical Can-Opener." The gentle souls of iDEATH indulge the narrator's eccentric need to write a book, but we can be fairly sure that it won't be a book of literary criticism. Such volumes, Brautigan might say, properly belong in the Forgotten Works.

I have certainly not floated with Brautigan here. I have used my critical can-opener, such as it is, and have tried not to read Brautigan's books as mystery novels. As I've said, I think it's necessary to look at Brautigan's work without either uncritical adulation or unsympathetic condescension. Jonathan Yardley, whom I've already cited a couple of times as an example of the latter attitude, begins his review of *The Abortion* by quoting a bookstore-owner friend of his (not, surely, the man from "Sea Sea Rider"), who allegedly told Yardley, "Every day, I expect to come in from lunch and find that the Brautigan cult has vanished in my absence."[2] Poof! And Brautigan will be gone, to the vast relief of Mr. Yardley and his friend.

I don't think so. I believe that Brautigan is a writer of both talent and substance—an artist—and that he'll be around for a while, for quite a while. As the many parallels between Brautigan's books and such recent, influential nonfiction works as Reich's *The Greening*

183

of America, Mungo's *Total Loss Farm*, Toffler's *Future Shock*, and Roszak's *The Making of a Counter Culture* suggest, Brautigan's thematic concerns seem especially relevant today. We might also note here Brautigan's apparent interest in and affinity with such contemporary music groups or performers as The Grateful Dead, The Jefferson Airplane, The Mamas and the Papas (all of which he mentions favorably in poems), The Beatles, Bob Dylan, Paul Simon. In each of his novels, as well as in many of his poems and stories, Brautigan is concerned with the problem of finding a personal "good world" to live in in the midst of a dehumanized society. It could surely be said that the authors and performers I've just mentioned and Brautigan would all agree with what Henry Miller says is the goal of life at Big Sur (or anywhere): ". . . not a bigger and better America but a world made for man."[3] Perhaps it could even be said that this is the chief goal of our time.

Despite the contentions of some of Brautigan's reviewers, Brautigan does not make this goal of "a world made for man" seem easy to achieve. Brautigan is sometimes sentimental but never fatuous. Of his four novels, *The Abortion* ends inconclusively; the narrator and Vida are snugly shacked up in Berkeley, in a house they share with Foster and a Pakistani graduate student, but at least something of the narrator's tendency toward withdrawn hermithood persists. Both *A Confederate General from Big Sur* and *Trout Fishing in America* conclude with the narrator's recognition that paradise has not been regained, that the "good world" is unattainable; in the former, the failure seems to stem from Jesse's inability to handle all the "life" that's been "thrown" at him in Big Sur, while in *Trout Fishing in America*, more convincingly perhaps, the problem seems to lie

184

in American society itself, which is depicted as inimical to the gentle life the narrator seeks. Only in *In Watermelon Sugar*, where the narrator begins by declaring, "I have a gentle life"(1), does this "good world" seem attainable. And the good world of that novel, iDEATH, is sharply qualified: first, by the fantasy terms of the book, by the fact that iDEATH is ultimately a state of mind rather than an actual condition; second, by the subdued, almost emotionless tone of the narrator. An awful lot—creativity and passion, as well as progress and materialism—has to be heaped on the Forgotten Work to achieve that gentle life. It don't come easy.

Although Brautigan is often a very funny writer, he is not finally an optimistic one. But then neither were most of our famous American "funnymen" of the past—from Mark Twain through James Thurber. Like any humorist, Brautigan gets much of his comic effect from a quick perception of incongruities. The world of his books is largely populated with social misfits who can't or won't adjust to the society around them. It's a pretty sad fictive world, when you come right down to it. It's a lonely world too; in my view, Brautigan is one of the major chroniclers of the loneliness of American experience. There are disproportionate numbers of solitary old people in Brautigan's world—the "Heap" in *Confederate General*, Mrs. Charles Fine Adams in *The Abortion*, the nice old lady who hires the narrator to do odd jobs in *Trout Fishing in America*, to mention only a few. There are also many, many born losers, loners, screwballs, screw-ups, and ineffectual rebels: ". . . the sailors who can't get laid, . . . the immobile visionaries, and the poor sick people . . ."(*Confederate General*, 42).

Whether he secludes himself in the library for losers

or whether he roams the Western states seeking the spirit of Trout Fishing in America, the autobiographical narrator of Brautigan's novels, stories, and poems tends to identify with these outsiders, cast-offs, and losers. Throughout Brautigan's work, the autobiographical persona can be described in Vida's phrase as one "not at home in the world" (*Abortion*, 52). Characteristically, the narrator of Brautigan's books feels nostalgic about the past—his own childhood and/or the American past; he looks back to a simpler time, a simpler world, when it was (or seemed to be) easier to control the terms of one's life, to find a "good world." We should remember that the narrator of *The Abortion* describes an unsuccessful writer named "Richard Brautigan" as a person looking "as if he would be more at home in another era"(28)—more at home in the American dawn of Lewis and Clark, perhaps, or even among the apparent childhood certainties of World War II.

Brautigan's preoccupation with the American mythic past—the predominance of nostalgia and elegy in his work—should remind us that the themes he explores are not only pertinent to the 1960s and 1970s; they are some of the central concerns of American literature. And Brautigan, as I've said, is very much in the American grain. In one way or another, virtually all of our major writers have "gone to look for America," like the man in Paul Simon's song, like the characters in *Trout Fishing in America.*

Brautigan has many affinities with older American writers. In my opinion, some of the most important are with Whitman, Thoreau, Henry Miller, Kenneth Patchen, Jack Kerouac, Mark Twain, William Carlos Williams, and Ernest Hemingway—especially with the last three. Aside from their American origins, Mark Twain, Wil-

186

liams, and Hemingway have one very important thing in common: all three had wonderful ears for the sounds and rhythms of American English. So does Brautigan; whatever else one might say about Brautigan's characters, their dialogue is always just right—we believe in their language even if we don't always quite believe in them. From Mark Twain—in whose centennial year he was born—Brautigan appears to have inherited a gift of rambling, yarn-spinning narrative energy. Brautigan's narrative style shows frequent similarities to the American Tall Tale tradition, in which there is generally a balance between wild exaggeration or distortion, on the one hand, and realistic circumstantial detail, on the other. From Dr. Williams, like so many of his contemporaries, Brautigan seems to have learned to see, to observe precisely, and to bring the apparently trivial or commonplace alive and thereby to raise it above banality. In addition, Brautigan would seem to have been influenced by Williams' sharp sense of the contrast between the undisturbed rhythms of Nature and man's disruptive, self-destructive lack of harmony with Nature's rhythms. These lines from *Patterson* could almost serve as an epigraph for all of Brautigan's work, tying together such diverse strands as *Please Plant This Book* and *Trout Fishing in America:* "But Spring shall come and flowers will bloom/and man must chatter of his doom . . ."[4]

Brautigan's relationship to Hemingway is complex and seems to be almost obsessive. Aside from several explicit references to Hemingway, Brautigan's work contains, I believe, at least a dozen conscious or unconscious specific echoes of Hemingway. The novelist Reynolds Price, who is almost exactly the same age as Brautigan, has recently asserted that Hemingway put his mark on

187

virtually all American writers of his (and Brautigan's) generation, even those (like Price himself) who did not particularly admire Hemingway when they were growing up and first starting to write. "For how many writers born in the twenties and thirties," Price asks, "can Hemingway not have been a breathing Mount Rushmore?"[5] Obviously, Brautigan and Hemingway share a deep feeling for fishing, for outdoor life, for Nature, and an almost religious sense of the curative powers of the simple life close to the earth and the water. Both are interested in the ceremonial, ritualistic possibilities of this simple outdoor life. But, beyond these relationships, they might seem to be almost totally contrasting figures: Hemingway with his interest in warfare and in physical combat of all sorts; Brautigan with his quest for an aggressionless, gentle life—Papa with his *machismo*, Richard with his little seed-packet poems. Perhaps the aspect of Hemingway which Brautigan most responds to finally is that quality of holding on—that stoicism—which pervades both "Big Two Hearted River" and *The Sun Also Rises* (both of which Brautigan echoes a couple of times). In Brautigan's world, grace under pressure becomes learning "strength through gentleness."

I'm not really trying to put Brautigan in the ring with Mr. Hemingway. Brautigan would not only disapprove of my critical can-opener, but also of the whole idea of ranking him or rating him as a writer. Brautigan tends to disparage his own achievements. For example, in the two part story, "Fame in California/1964," he makes fun of himself and virtually jeers at what he calls the "feathery crowbar" of fame (*Revenge of the Lawn*, 132). Yet, quite apart from the large sales and succession of new editions of his books, there is evidence that Brautigan is making a real impact on American culture, on various levels. As I've mentioned, he has already been paid the left-handed compliment of parody twice in prestigious publications. (Not to mention all the compliments of imitation he must be receiving these days in college creative writing classrooms and elsewhere). A very good recent novel, Tom Robbins' *Another Roadside Attraction* (Doubleday, 1971, makes explicit reference to *Trout Fishing in America*. I don't know whether this item really pertains to Brautigan's growing fame, but I must also mention that a very recent issue of *Life* magazine (17 March 1972) contains a mammoth double-page photograph of 1,900 anglers jammed together in a stream in Missouri, fishing for 7,800 trout. (Brautigan, I like to think, would enjoy the enumeration, with his fondness for lists and numbers, though probably he would disapprove of the evident rounding-off of figures.) Finally—although this might be incidental too—I have before me as I write these words a packet containing marigold seeds, which was sent to me by, of all people, the circulation director of *Time* magazine; he wants me to subscribe to *Time*. Except that the packet does not have a poem written on it, it could be a portion of Brautigan's *Please Plant This Book*. There are signs of Brautigan's direct or indirect influence on our culture everywhere.

All in all, it looks like Jonathan Yardley and his friend will have to wait quite a while for Brautigan's literary demise. But what of Brautigan's probable future works? If we accept the dates Brautigan gives for the composition of his major books, his four novels, then he hasn't written a sustained work in more than five years: *Trout Fishing in America* (1961), *Confederate General* (1963), *In Watermelon Sugar* (1964), *The Abortion* (1966). Perhaps he feels that he has tapped out the vein that produced these four books, since, as I've said, all four of them are in a sense variations on the same general theme—the shy loner trying to find a "good world" in the inhospitable America of the 1960s. One of Brautigan's most recently published stories, "The World War I Los Angeles Airplane"(1971), suggests that possibly Brautigan might be turning more and more to nonautobiographical materials. Whether this story indicates a trend or not, however, its publication is still a very encouraging sign, for any Brautigan admirer, because it is one of his best stories.

We can be fairly sure, I think, that Brautigan, at thirty-seven, is a long way from being written out. Any writer of thirty-seven (or any young writer) is hard to sum up or speculate on. Who knows what he'll do next? Brautigan is even more difficult to generalize about than most writers, though, because it is impossible to separate his major strengths from his weaknesses. Perhaps what Daniel Hoffman says of Edgar Allen Poe is also true of Brautigan: "We can't get his genius without his fudge, or his fudge without his genius. Nor is it a foregone conclusion which is which."[6] Tentatively in the fudge category I'd place Brautigan's relative lack of interest in character development, his intermittent unsureness of structure, his occasional sentimentality, his overindulgence in, on the one hand, commonplace incidents and, on the other, merely whimsical fantasy. In the opposite category, I'd place Brautian's good (often brilliant) eye for details, his ear for American English, his sense of comic incongruity, his ability to be gentle without being insipid, his ability to balance realism and fantasy, his narrative energy, his fresh—sometimes startling—perceptions. Even if I don't accept the idea of Brautigan's books as "mystery novels," obviously there is a final mystery to Brautigan's talents—as there is to any artist's. After all is said about his relationship to past American writers and about his presentation of themes that seem relevant to American experience in the 1970s, Brautigan's originality remains. He has looked at what you and I have looked at, but he has seen things that we haven't. Who could imagine the Cleveland Wrecking Yard before Brautigan showed us that it waits, inevitably, at the sad end of the American pastoral dream?

More genius than fudge, clearly. But these categories obviously overlap, and, as Hoffman says, it's not a foregone conclusion which works belong to which category. It will be fun to see what Brautigan's next book is like—and the one after that too.

Footnotes to Preface:

[1] Bruce Cook, *The Beat Generation* (New York: Charles Scribner's Sons, 1971), pp. 207-8.

[2] Cf. Brautigan's poem, "Yeah, There Was Always Going to Be a June 5, 1968," about Robert Kennedy's assassination (in *Rommel Drives on Deep into Egypt*, p. 49).

[3] Cf. Brautigan's story, "Forgiven," in which the narrator asks Richard Brautigan's forgiveness for encroaching on his literary turf (*Revenge of the Lawn*, p. 167).

[4] Quoted by Cook, p. 207.

[5] See the headnote and postscript to "The Lost Chapters of *Trout Fishing in America*" (in *Revenge of the Lawn*, pp. 37, 41).

[6] Anonymous review of *Revenge of the Lawn*, *New Republic*, 22 January 1972, p. 29.

[7] *Pill Versus Springhill Mine Disaster*, p. 66.

Footnotes to Chapter One: The Poems

[1] David Meltzer, ed., *The San Francisco Poets* (New York: Ballantine Books, 1971), p. 294.

[2] In a review of *Rommel Drives Deep into Egypt,* Kate Rose says, "Sometimes I just can't see his images . . ." (*Minnesota Review,* X [1970], 116). I think this is the sort of thing she means. It's hard to see (imagine) what the figurative sewing machine in this poem is experiencing or feeling.

[3] Jonathan Yardley, "Still Loving," *New Republic,* 20 March 1971, p. 24.

[4] Bruce Cook, *The Beat Generation* (New York: Charles Scribner's Sons, 1971), p. 206.

[5] Of course, silence can be very effective *in* a poem (if not as the whole poem). In "Karma Repair Kit" *(The Pill,* 8), Brautigan skillfully builds up to the blank final section of the poem.

[6] Jerome Rothenberg's wonderful anthology, *Technicians of the Sacred* (Garden City: Doubleday and Co., 1968), is, among many other things, an attempt to reassert the ancient role of the poet as priest-magician.

[7] Quoted in Hunter Davies, *The Beatles* (New York: Dell, 1969), p. 321.

[8] Cook, p. 208

[9] Meltzer, p. 293.

Footnotes to Chapter Two:
Revenge of the Lawn

[1] Anatole Broyard, "Weeds and Four-Leaf Clovers," *New York Times*, 15 November 1971, p. 37.

[2] Mark Twain, "The Story of the Old Ram," in *Collected Stories of Mark Twain* (New York: Bantam Books, 1958), p. 81. The story first appeared in *Roughing It* (1872).

[3] Mark Twain, "How to Tell a Story," in George Perkins, ed., *The Theory of the American Novel* (New York: Holt, Rinehart, and Winston, 1970), pp. 106–7.

[4] Josephine Hendin, Review of *Revenge of the Lawn*, *New York Times Book Review*, 16 January 1972, p. 22.

[5] Jonathan Yardley more or less takes this position in his review of *The Abortion*, "Still Loving," *New Republic*, 20 March 1971, pp. 24–5. In contrast to the title and spirit of Yardley's article, Miss Hendin says

that the kind of "detachment" Brautigan advocates "permits you to be kind but never loving . . ." (p. 22).

⁶ Broyard, for example, criticizes the ending of "A Short History of Oregon" for being heavy-handed (p. 37).

⁷ Hendin, p. 7.

⁸ Broyard, who obviously has very mixed feelings about Brautigan's work, points out that "Brautigan has a good feeling for the American past . . ." (p. 37).

⁹ Besides Lingeman's *Don't You Know There's a War on?* (New York: Paperback Library, 1971), George Frazier's witty article, "Welcome Back to the Forties" (*Esquire,* October 1971, pp. 98f.), indicates that Brautigan is hardly the only person of his generation who feels nostalgic about the World War II years.

¹⁰ Brautigan uses doors symbolically as leading to knowledge or communication frequently throughout *Revenge of the Lawn.* In "One Afternoon in 1939," for example, the story he tells his four-year-old daughter about himself at that age is described "as a kind of Christopher Columbus door" to the child's understanding of her father (117). As I've already said, the opulent door of "The Wild Birds of Heaven" is used ironically, leading to the blacksmith's shop where Mr. Henley is stripped of his shadow. It's appropriate that in the amusing self-deprecatory sketch, "Fame in California/1964" (Part 1), when the narrator is told that he is being used as a character in a novel being written by a friend, his only role in the book is to open a door (132).

¹¹ Broyard, p. 37.

¹² Hendin, p. 22.

¹³ "The World War I Los Angeles Airplane" appeared originally in the *New American Review,* Number 12 (New York: Simon and Schuster, 1971). The stories in *Revenge of the Lawn* are not arranged chronologically, either in order of composition or publication. Nor, although some similar stories are grouped together (e.g., three consecutive stories— "A Short History of Religion in California," "April in God-Damn," and "One Afternoon in 1939" (111–17)—concern Brautigan's daughter), does there seem to be a discernible overall organization of the stories.

¹⁴ Quoted in Bruce Cook, *The Beat Generation* (New York: Charles Scribner's Sons, 1971), p. 208.

Footnotes to Chapter Three:
The Abortion

[1] *New York Times Book Review*, 6 June 1971, pp. 7, 14.

[2] After completing this chapter, I came upon another Brautigan parody: Garrison Keillor, "Ten Stories for Mr. Richard Brautigan and Other Stories," in, of all places, *New Yorker* (18 March 1972, p. 37). In so far as Keillor's parody takes off any specific Brautigan works, it seems to be based on the short short stories in *Revenge of the Lawn*. It strikes me as a singularly feeble effort, but, once again, the fact that sophisticated *New Yorker* should publish *any* Brautigan parody is an important indication of his growing fame.

[3] V. S. Pritchett, Review of Walker Percy's *Love in the Ruins* and Jerzy Kosinski's *Being There*, *New York Review of Books*, 1 July 1971, p. 15.

[4] Jonathan Yardley, "Still Loving," *New Republic*, 20 March 1971, p. 24.

Footnotes to Chapter Four:
A Confederate General from Big Sur

[1] Leslie Fiedler, *Love and Death in the American Novel*, revised edition (New York: Dell, 1968), pp. 5–12.

[2] Jack Kerouac, *Big Sur* (New York: Bantam, 1963), p. 55.

[3] Henry Miller, *Big Sur and the Oranges of Hieronymus Bosch* (New York: New Directions, 1957), p. 30.

[4] Readers interested in such matters might compare Brautigan's treatment of the Battle of the Wilderness to the eye-witness accounts of Robert Robertson (G.A.R.) and J. B. Polley (C.S.A.), excerpted in Otto Eisenschiml and Ralph Newman, *The American Illiad* (New York: Grosset & Dunlap, 1956), pp. 553f. Polley's narrative appears to be a possible direct source of Brautigan's account.

[5] Kenneth Patchen, *The Journal of Albion Moonlight* (Norfolk, Conn.: New Directions, 1941), p. 313.

[6] Miller, p. 13.

[7] Miller, p. 18.

[8] Allen Ginsberg, "After Dead Souls," *Empty Mirror* (New York: Corinth Books, 1960), p. 31.

[9] *The Complete Stories of Mark Twain* (New York: Bantam, 1958), p. 81.

Footnotes to Chapter Five:
In Watermelon Sugar

[1] Nora Ephron and Susan Emiston, "Bob Dylan Interview," in Jonathan Eisen, ed., *The Age of Rock 2* (New York: Random House, 1970), p. 67. Specifically, Dylan is talking about the way old ballads—"Lord Edward," "Barbara Allen"—seem full of life and myth.

[2] It's also possible that Brautigan's tigers were influenced by the aggressive, instinctive "lions of fire" in Kenneth Patchen's poem, "The Lions of Fire Shall Have Their Hunting" *(Selected Poems of Kenneth Patchen* (New York: New Directions, 1957), pp. 85–6).

[3] R. D. Laing, *The Politics of Experience* (New York: Ballantine Books, 1968), p. 150. iDEATH might also be compared to the name of the San Francisco rock group, The Grateful Dead, with which Brautigan is certainly familiar. (See his poem, "The Day They Busted the Grateful Dead," in *The Pill* (104).) Michael Lydon says of the Dead, ". . . they are, or desire to become, the grateful dead. Grateful Dead may mean whatever you like it to mean, life-in-death, ego death, reincarnation, the joy of the mystic vision *(Rock Folk* [New York: Dial Press, 1971], p. 118).

[4] Theodore Roszak, *The Making of a Counter Culture* (Garden City: Doubleday Anchor Books, 1969), p. 75.

⁵ *Collected Poems of W. B. Yeats* (New York: The MacMillan Co., 1959), p. 187.

⁶ "The Second Coming," *Collected Poems*, p. 184.

⁷ Thomas Lask, "Move over Mr. Tolstoy," *New York Times*, 30 March 1971, p. 33.

⁸ Thomas McGuane, Review of *Trout Fishing in America*, *The Pill Versus the Springhill Mine Disaster*, and *In Watermelon Sugar*, *New York Times Book Review*, 15 February 1970, p. 49.

⁹ McGuane suggests a comparison between *In Watermelon Sugar* and Herbert Read's *The Green Child*, but aside from the very general similarity of two well-realized fantasy worlds, the books don't seem much alike to me.

¹⁰ Charles Reich, *The Greening of America* (New York: Random House, 1970), p. 225.

¹¹ Reich, p. 391.

¹² Raymond Mungo, *Total Loss Farm* (New York: E. P. Dutton, 1970), p. 128.

¹³ Mungo, p. 148. Another important book that is pertinent to *In Watermelon Sugar* (as well as to *Total Loss Farm*) is Alvin Toffler's *Future Shock* (New York: Bantam Books, 1971). Toffler would certainly include both Brautigan and Mungo in his criticism of those writers who create regressive utopias depicting "a pre-industrial way of life—small, close to the earth, built on farming and handcraft" (p. 466).

Footnotes to Chapter Six:
Trout Fishing in America

[1] I am omitting from consideration the two so-called "Lost Chapters of *Trout Fishing in America*," which have been reprinted in *Revenge of the Lawn*. Whether or not one accepts Brautigan's contention that he rewrote these chapters about eight years after losing them, I don't think they belong in a discussion of *Trout Fishing in America*. First of all, they seem to me markedly inferior to most of the material in *Trout Fishing in America*; second, they don't fit into the structure of the book at all.

[2] Quoted in J. Anthony Lukas, *The Barnyard Epithet* (New York: Harper & Row, 1970), p. 65.

[3] Robert Adams, "Brautigan Was Here," *New York Review of Books*, 22 April 1971, pp. 25, 24.

[4] John Clayton, "Richard Brautigan: The Politics of Woodstock,"

New American Review, Number 11 (New York: Simon and Schuster, 1971), p. 64.

[5] Although he attacks Brautigan somewhat ferociously for the escapist implications of his work, Clayton at least doesn't patronize him; he is perhaps the main exception to my generalization. Adams, even though he makes several sharp appreciative points, does seem to me to condescend to Brautigan's work (see, for example, his discussion of *In Watermelon Sugar* [pp. 24–5]).

[6] Clayton, p. 60.

[7] This parenthetical aside is not entirely facetious. On his record, *Listening to Richard Brautigan,* Brautigan reads an episode from *Trout Fishing in America,* "The Hunchback Trout," with the sound of rushing water very prominent in the background; the effect is very striking, as if the book were indeed written to be read alongside a fast-moving trout stream.

[8] Since Brautigan uses the title phrase, Trout Fishing in America, in various ways, there's inevitably going to be a risk of confusion in my use of that phrase. Throughout this chapter, *Trout Fishing in America* refers to the title of Brautigan's book; Trout Fishing in America refers to the mythic figure whose spirit pervades the book or to the "good world" the characters in it seek; trout fishing in America refers to the activity of fishing for trout in the U.S.A.

[9] Clayton, p. 57.

[10] Thomas McGuane, Review of *Trout Fishing in America, The Pill Versus the Springhill Mine Disaster,* and *In Watermelon Sugar, New York Times Book Review,* 15 February 1970, p. 49.

[11] Thomas Pynchon, *The Crying of Lot 49* (Philadelphia: J. B. Lippincott Company, 1966), p. 179.

[12] Clayton, p. 56. In the last few pages of his essay (pp. 65–8), Clayton makes his objections to Brautigan's vision most explicit.

[13] Josephine Hendin, Review of *Revenge of the Lawn, New York Times Book Review,* 6 January 1972, p. 7.

[14] Brautigan's aversion to the wanton destruction of vermin or predators gains additional force if we recall the ugly recent news stories about the widespread killing of eagles and coyotes from helicopters. (See, for instance, William M. Blair, "Shooting of 500 Eagles Described by a Pilot," *The New York Times,* 3 August 1971, p. 9.) Ironically, not only the coyote but even the American bald eagle has become a kind of domestic Viet Cong to be searched for and destroyed by helicopter.

[15] There's no way to work the point in neatly, I'm afraid, but I should at least note here that another pervasive element in *Trout Fishing in America* consists of more than a dozen references to excrement (human or animal) and outhouses. It is probably this aspect of the book that Adams has in mind when he makes the curious remark that *Trout Fishing in America* relies to some extent on "obscenity for easy effects" (p. 25). One significance of these unsavory references is to emphasize the idea of a crowded America buried in its own waste; we should recall Brautigan's listing of "suffocating [in] human excrement" as one of the "natural ways" for a trout to die (29).

[16] Adams, p. 25.

Footnotes to Conclusion:

[1] Robert James Toye, Letter to the Editor, *New York Times Book Review*, 27 February 1972, p. 24.

[2] Jonathan Yardley, "Still Loving," *New Republic*, 20 March 1971, p. 24.

[3] Henry Miller, *Big Sur and the Oranges of Hieronymus Bosch* (New York: New Directions, 1957), p. 256.

[4] William Carlos Williams, *Patterson*, Book Two, Part III (New York: New Directions, 1963), p. 95.

[5] Reynolds Price, "For Ernest Hemingway," *New American Review*, Number 14 (New York: Simon and Schuster, 1972), p. 52.

[6] Daniel Hoffman, *Poe Poe Poe Poe Poe Poe Poe* (Garden City: Doubleday, 1972), p. x.

Bibliography

Here are the editions of Brautigan's books that I have used in this study:

Trout Fishing in America. New York: Dell, 1967.

A Confederate General from Big Sur. New York: Grove Press, 1968.

The Pill Versus the Springhill Mine Disaster. San Francisco: Four Seasons Foundation, 1968.

In Watermelon Sugar. San Francisco: Four Seasons Foundation, 1968.

Rommel Drives on Deep into Egypt. New York: Dell, 1970.

The Abortion. New York: Simon and Schuster, 1971.

Revenge of the Lawn. New York: Simon and Schuster, 1971.

Most of the critical articles on Brautigan's work have not seemed to me very helpful. Here are the ones I think are the most useful:

Adams, Robert. "Brautigan Was Here," *New York Review of Books,* 22 April 1971, pp. 24–5.

Clayton, John. "Richard Brautigan: The Politics of Woodstock," in *New American Review,* Number 11. New York: Simon and Schuster, 1971, pp. 56–68.

Hendin, Josephine. Review of *Revenge of the Lawn, New York Times Book Review,* 16 January 1972, pp. 7, 22.

McGuane, Thomas. Review of *Trout Fishing in America, The Pill Versus the Springhill Mine Disaster,* and *In Watermelon Sugar, New York Times Book Review,* 15 February 1970, pp. 49–50.

In addition, even though the following books are not primarily concerned with Brautigan's work (four of them don't even refer to him specifically), all five provide useful perspective for looking at Richard Brautigan:

Cook, Bruce. *The Beat Generation.* New York: Charles Scribner's Sons, 1971.

Mungo, Raymond. *Total Loss Farm*. New York: E. P. Dutton, 1970.

Reich, Charles. *The Greening of America*. New York: Random House, 1970.

Roszak, Theodore. *The Making of a Counter Culture*. Garden City: Doubleday Anchor Books, 1969.

Toffler, Alvin. *Future Shock*. New York: Bantam Books, 1971.

☐ **TO BE YOUNG IN BABYLON**
by Tom Seligson

Tom Seligson has traveled into the center of the agony of young America and returned to describe, honestly and sensitively, the teenage political rebels, the exiles, the outlaws, the confused youth. The young Indians of Standing Rock and Alcatraz, the blacks of Peoria, working-class white youth in Erie and Chicago, middle-class kids in New York and Mississippi, the Chicanos of California . . . all are here. Despite the violence of the young, their nihilism and sexual confusion, Seligson writes with an ultimate faith in this generation. If you are concerned about the future of America, **To Be Young in Babylon** is essential reading. (66-731, $1.25)

☐ **TERRACIDE: America's Destruction Of Her Living Environment**
by Ron M. Linton

Ron Linton is one of a new breed of men—today's environmentalists—a concerned, outspoken group of professionals who are attempting to combat the disastrous consequences of the misuse of our precious natural environment. **Terracide** is both a vital exploration of our dispoiled urban and country life and a startling testimony to the effect this destruction has on our daily lives. (66-540, $1.25)

If you are unable to obtain these books from your local dealer, they may be ordered directly from the publisher. Please allow 4 weeks for delivery.

WARNER PAPERBACK LIBRARY
P.O. Box 3
Farmingdale, New York 11735

Please send me the books I have checked.
I am enclosing payment plus 10c per copy to cover postage and handling.

Name ....

Address ....

City .... State .... Zip ....

_____ Please send me your free mail order catalog